LLOYD PURVES
on
CLOSING SALES

LLOYD PURVES

on

CLOSING SALES

Lloyd Purves

Parker Publishing Company, Inc. West Nyack, N.Y.

© 1979 *by*

Parker Publishing Company, Inc.

West Nyack, New York

Reward Edition . . . . . . September 1980

Library of Congress Cataloging in Publication Data

Purves, Lloyd
    Lloyd Purves on closing sales.

    Includes index.
    1. Selling.   I.   Title.
HF5438.25.P873   658.85   78-15144

Printed in the United States of America

Also by the Author:

HOW TO MAKE $10,000 A YEAR EXTRA FROM "LOST SALES"

What This Book Will Do for You

There is one puzzling thing that I have learned above all else in over thirty years of training and working with some of the best salesmen in the business. It is this: The closing—the most important part of the whole sales endeavor— is often the most troublesome area for many otherwise competent and able salesmen. I have seen brilliant, hard-working men conduct excellent presentations then walk away empty-handed because they faltered and agonized at the closing. There can be no more disheartening spectacle.

This need never happen to you. This book provides powerful, tested methods and techniques that I have perfected and used to close millions of dollars worth of big commission sales. You will also see how other salesmen have achieved success and earned magnificent sums of money by utilizing these sales closing secrets. The ideas in this book can be a gold mine for you.

Nothing exceeds the cold authority of a closed sale. No one commands more respect than the salesman who knows how and when to close a sale. He has the admiration of his peers, his customers, and his competitors. He is the man who keeps all those lovely greenbacks in circulation. It is a good feeling, believe me.

This book deals in fresh ideas that close sales. It digs into new information to give tried and proven techniques additional closing fire and power. Sales closing procedures are explained in a clear, concise manner, ready for you to put into action at once. This book is an effective tool to keep seasoned salesmen closing more and bigger sales.

The experience and methods disclosed in this book can put you in the front ranks with other winners and keep you there. For instance, you will see:

- How Bill Morrow maintained personal control and closed a $200,000 sale on the spot. (Chapter 1)
- How Kermit Fuller used domination to close a sale worth $150,000 in commissions. (Chapter 1)
- How Fred Buckner closed a million dollar life insurance sale by finding an area of agreement and put a $20,000 commission in his pocket. (Chapter 8)

- How John Chrysler closed his sale with the prestige appeal and made himself $50,000 in the bargain. (**Chapter 15**)
- How Miké Halstead closed his sale when the prospect wouldn't talk and thereby created a lot of repeat business. (**Chapter 18**)
- How Jennifer Norton won a position on the board of directors of her company by closing a sale when the customer couldn't make up his mind. (**Chapter 16**)
- How Paul Hite earned PMs and commissions of $2,250 when he knocked out a put-off and closed his sale with product knowledge. (**Chapter 3**)
- How Harold Messerly earned $9,000 by closing a real estate deal on a minor point. (**Chapter 7**)
- How an industrial salesman utilized the emotional appeal of fear to close a sale and collect $25,000 in commissions. (**Chapter 10**)

The secrets of many other vibrant salesmen are revealed for you. The proof that you can double and redouble your closed sales, no matter what your field, is here for you.

When you have mastered the techniques and know-how in such chapters as

How to Close by Domination
How to Close Under Stiff Competition
How to Close in the Face of Price Objections
How to Close when the Prospect Won't Talk
Techniques to Use to Close Under Intimidation Tactics
How to Close the Big Shooter

and the other equally powerful chapters in this book, it will be obvious to you that the closing can be the most exciting and stimulating part of your sales activities. Using the expertise in this book you will move easily and quickly through each sales presentation to a strong closing. That is the way it has worked for me and other salesmen I've known and admired for a long time. That is the way it will work for you.

A great salesman once said that nothing happens until somebody sells something. Of course, he is right. It is not too difficult in a highly skilled and technically oriented society to create or manufacture something. However, it is not always a simple matter to sell that something. And nobody sells anything until the sale is closed. The closed sale is what this book is all about.

Lloyd Purves

Contents

How using the choice method makes it easy for the customer to say
yes—How to use a choice to get the buyer to close the sale for
you—How a choice demands a decision—How to limit your
choices for a quick closing—How to know when to close on a
choice.

How to use words that create strong desire—How to close sales
with an economy of words—Beware killer words—Tom Field's
confusion index—How to stick with fast action words that close
the sale.

How to use profit as the great motivator—How to tell profit stories
that close the sale—How to close on your own profit
contribution—How to close by demonstrating profitability.

How to use "pride of ownership" to close—How to close with the
prestige appeal—How to close with the security benefit appeal—
How to close with the "leadership" benefiit—Don't be stingy with
the goodies—*You* get fringe benefits also.

Make a hero of the wishy-washy type—How Ray Hunter got his
buyer off the fence—How to close this type with proof—How to
make the decision for the customer who can't make up his mind—
Everybody's ahead when you close Mr. Indecision.

Take advantage of this: The tougher they are the more they want
their ego pampered—How to find and use honest compliments to
close your sale—Ignoring the ego can shoot you down—How to
beat the competition by using the ego appeal to close your sale—
Ego is not the same as conceit—How to use your own ego to close
more sales—Concentrate your own ego on the closed sale.

down by restating key points—How to use your departure to make sure the sale stays closed—How to check on the order to make sure the sale stays closed—How to use credit information to make sure that your sale stays closed—Promise what you can deliver and deliver what you promise—Be available after the sale is closed—How to get others to help keep your sale closed—How to lock in your closed sale when it is made.

Start closing at the first contact—How to use objections to make a power play—Obtain little confirmations—How to use tie-downs—Answer questions with questions—Avoid cliches that steal fire power—How to use command power to explode your closing power—How to *insist on and win* the right decision—How to make the customer like aggressive you—How to maintain a strong closing posture.

LLOYD PURVES
on
CLOSING SALES

1

How to Close by Domination

One fact that you should not forget is this: Either you will dominate a sales situation or your customer will. You may close an occasional sale if the customer dominates you, but don't count on it. Even though a customer or prospect likes and needs what you are selling, he doesn't want to buy it from a salesman who can easily be side-tracked or intimidated.

CONTROL OR BE CONTROLLED

So you can be sure that on every sales call you make you are going to be in control or you are going to be controlled. One way leads to closed sales; the other way leads to the human scrap heap. Fortunately, you have a choice. Now, let's discuss some elements which will insure that you establish and maintain control of your sales efforts from the first word of your presentation to the closed sale.

The number one thing to fix in your mind is that domination is not senseless brute force. It is more than that. It is a subtle power employed by the well-prepared salesman. It is the fire of a businessman who has set his sights on a goal and who refuses to be thrown off course or intimidated.

There is nothing immoral or obscene about using personal domination to close a sale. Indeed, *it is what your customer wants.* He is not about to entrust his business, his resources, to a wishy-washy salesman. He would be short-sighted and foolish to do so. What he wants and needs is your expertise clearly and forcefully presented. He is looking for the help of a strong, dominant salesman who will contribute to his success and show him how to make more money, or otherwise benefit. And who can fault his logic?

While we're on this crucial subject, make a little note on this too: you will be tested on practically every sales call. Buyers have a way of decimating indecisive salesmen. It may seem cruel to the uninitiated, but the truth is that only dominant salesmen survive and flourish. It is also true that only dominant salesmen have much to offer the customer. With that in mind, let's deal with some specific ways you can use domination to close worthwhile sales and to serve your customers and society most worthily in the process.

HOW TO USE DOMINATION TO CONVINCE

Bill Morrow was ushered into Mr. Samuel Dykes' office by Mr. Dykes' secretary. Mr. Dykes greeted Bill cordiallly, and then introduced Russell Newhouse, whom Bill quickly learned was Mr. Dykes' heir apparent. Mr. Dykes was operating a large family-owned textile mill at an age when most men are retired and counting their laurels. Unfortunately, there was no family member to carry on the business, so Mr. Dykes had faced the obvious and was grooming his replacement. Mr. Newhouse was that man.

Bill went to work as soon as the introductions had been properly and courteously acknowledged. He spread his presentation on the desk before Mr. Dykes and began to review and emphasize key features of the many-faceted and sophisticated machine that Mr. Dykes had shown an interest in on an earlier call. Bill was meticulous. There was a $200,000 sale at stake.

But when Bill detailed the increased production and clear-cut pattern definition possible on the new machine because of its computer assisted automatic operation, Russell Newhouse protested, "But how about down time on a complicated machine like that? The cost would be prohibitive!"

Bill explained that the piece of equipment was used by a number of leading manufacturers and that down time was minimal. Further, his company maintained a full-time service department for any emergencies that might arise. Mr. Newhouse looked skeptical, but he did relax a little.

But when Bill pointed out the super-efficient needle bar, Russell Newhouse was out of his seat and worrying about "broken needles." Bill patiently reassured him.

For another ten minutes Bill endured interruption after interruption and objection on top of objection at every trivial excuse. It was obvious to Bill that Russell Newhouse was working overtime to prove to Mr. Dykes that he was the right choice to be the next president of Dykes' Textiles and Rugs, Incorporated. It was equally obvious that Bill was going to have to maintain control if he were to convince Mr. Dykes of the merit of his proposal.

Bill turned to Mr. Dykes and in a calm and persuasive voice said, "Mr. Dykes, you built this fine company by making the right decisions. You chose Mr. Newhouse as your successor. I'm sure that you have made an excellent choice. But it is obvious that the decision on this new equipment, which you badly need, must be yours alone. With that in mind, I wonder if Mr. Newhouse would be kind enough to leave us for a few minutes. I would like to make sure that all of your specifications have been met so that we can put this equipment on line for you without delay."

Mr. Dykes nodded. Mr. Newhouse excused himself with as much dignity and grace as he could muster.

The deal was soon consummated and then, at Bill's suggestion, Mr. Dykes called Newhouse back into his office. Bill tactfully explained the decision had been made, Mr. Dykes' reasons for making it, and then he said, "But we wanted your OK since you are the one who must live with this baby for a long time."

Of course, Russell Newhouse agreed with considerable enthusiasm.

Note two things: (1) Bill took drastic steps to keep control. (2) He took great pains to erase any future animosity by letting Mr. Newhouse save face. (When you have to knock somebody's teeth out in a case like this, it is always a good idea to do it as painlessly as possible.)

The chief item to note is that Bill used forceful domination in order to create an atmosphere in which he could convince Mr. Dykes that his machine was the one to buy and that now was the time to buy it. Ask yourself: Could he have closed the sale then and there if Mr. Newhouse had been permitted to grab the ball and dominate the interview?

Happily, it isn't often that you will have to resort to extreme brashness to keep control of your sale in order to drive your story home. Skillful, unobtrusive personal domination is strong stuff. It doesn't need be—indeed shouldn't be—crude and antagonistic. Bill Morrow was backed into a corner and forced to be rather blunt, but he did use considerable finesse and managed to leave everybody feeling good. And he did collect his $30,000 commission.

HOW TO USE DOMINATION TO ESTABLISH CONTROL

I have a friend who has sold, and continues to sell, millions of dollars worth of insurance every year. Most of his sales are made with the wife of his client, or prospect, present. Before he makes his presentation, Frank Atkins, my friend of long standing, has an ingenious routine he uses to establish control. He usually asks the wife to sit elsewhere once she is comfortably settled. Of course, he does this tactfully while offering some reason, however, trivial, for his request. Once she is again seated, he then asks her to check a few figures on the proposal he has prepared. Next he will ask the husband to loan him his pen, though he always has at least two tucked inside his own pocket. He continues along this tack until the man and his wife are subconsciously conditioned to follow his suggestions. Moreover, he employs the same discriminating tactics when he is selling insurance to a high-powered business executive. Frank's volume of paid cases is proof positive that human nature at all levels responds favorably to intelligent domination when applied with polite, firm skill. This kind of planned domination paves the way for Frank to convince his clients to buy. It enables Frank to maintain a high ratio of closed sales to calls. It will do as much for you.

When a well-meaning, fumbling salesman loses control, everybody loses. But when personal domination is studied, understood, planned, and practiced to effect conviction leading to closed sales, you and your customers benefit from a mutually rewarding business .saction.

HOW TO USE DOMINATION TO HOLD ATTENTION

Henry Pursley was trying to nail down his usual spring order from a large institutional food distributor. He had offered his firm's customary generous dating and bonus merchandise on such orders to be booked for early delivery. He had carefully prepared a three truckload order from past records of this distributor's performance. For several years such orders had been routinely picked up at the nearby plant of Henry's firm. But today Henry's customer was distracted and fuzzy. He left his office two or three times without explanation and generally seemed preoccupied. He admitted he wanted the datings, the discounts, and the free goods, but he couldn't sit still long enough to give Henry his undivided attention. When he arose to leave again, Henry arose with him and quietly pitched his tentative order into the waste basket. He headed for the door, but suddenly his buyer friend reverted to his old courteous, attentive self. He called Henry back, a few minor revisions were made in the order, and after warm handshakes were exchanged Henry left with his three truckload order. Of course, the distributor disposed of the merchandise and more, as Henry was certain he would do. The relationship between Henry and his customer is exemplary and Henry continues to write the kind of orders that help his customer realize his greatest potential.

What would have happened had Henry failed to exercise dominance to get and hold attention?

His firm would have been shipping small, less profitable orders every week. Henry would have spent unnecessary time watching and checking the distributor's inventory. The distributor would have had added freight costs, he would have lost his dating terms, his truckload discounts, and his bonus merchandise. Too, he would have been working on a short inventory and missing business because of "outs." All this, to say nothing of the inconvenience and the loss which the distributor's customers would have suffered had Henry been a lesser salesman. When you know your position is proper and your facts correct, you have every right, indeed, a profound obligation to maintain a dominant stance and command attention. If you do not, everybody loses. When you do, everybody wins.

There are other situations calling for a show of dominance in order to hold attention. One of the most disconcerting things that can happen to a man trying to make an impressive sales presentation is to be frequently interrupted by the phone, or by someone thoughtlessly barging in and out of the buyer's office. The most judicious way to handle this problem is to simply halt the presentation and explain that cooperation is necessary. If things are so disjointed that an exercise of personal dominance can't create a favorable atmosphere, it is better to gracefully excuse yourself and arrange a time when you can work without interruption. No matter how expert you may be, you can't close a sale when the buyer is distracted beyond tolerance. If you are to get the job done, you must be the dominant center of attention. Nothing less will suffice.

If a strong-willed, or temperamental customer is inclined to go off on a tangent with a barrage of totally unrelated (unrelated to your purpose, that is) statements, use your dominance like this: stop your presentation, or demonstration, until he is calm again. Don't be trapped into trying to compete with him on a volume basis. Say nothing until he runs down. Then, matter-of-factly pick up where you left off. Refuse to permit his attention to be riveted elsewhere. He will get the idea and go along with you to a satisfactory closing as your dominant action leads and guides him within the bounds of sweet reason.

When attention strays, strong experienced salesmen call upon dominance to control the buyer's attention until the sale is closed. Whatever the situation, you can fit a show of personal dominance into it and keep attention. It is nothing more than a happy accident if you close a sale while the buyer's mind is chasing butterflies.

HOW TO USE DOMINATION TO FORCE INVOLVEMENT

As an experienced salesman, you know that getting the customer involved is a great help in closing a sale. If your buyer friend is reluctant, don't merely ask him to take part. Use a bit of psychologically powered force. Hand him a sample. Let him see for himself how it works, tastes, smells, looks, and feels. If you are selling an intangible, give him a brochure, pamphlet, or some figures to examine. When you use personal domination to force involvement, you are putting the customer in a position to close the sale for you. You can't beat that with a ten foot stick!

HOW TO USE DOMINATION TO ESTABLISH AUTHORITY

As a well-qualified, capable salesman, you thoroughly know your product. You are cognizant of your firm's policies. You know what you can do and what you cannot do. This makes you the authority.

When your facts are disputed, doubt is expressed, or your customer is hazy, then is the time to assert your authority if you hope to close the sale. And if you've been out in the field more than half an hour, then you know that the salesman with authority is the one the customers will hand their business.

James Gifford, an OEM salesman from way back, expresses it this way. "I'm a specialist," says Jim, "and I make it my business to be an expert in my field. This puts me in a dominant light. I can answer questions, solve problems, make recommendations, and help my customers run a more profitable business. I couldn't do this, nor could I close many sales, if I didn't conduct myself as an authority."

Hiding your abilities is no way to close sales. Bringing them up front in a dominant, confident manner will establish you as an authority who deserves the business. Take your cue from James Gifford.

HOW TO USE DOMINATION TO WIN

There are still a few uninformed individuals who look upon a buyer-seller confrontation as a destructive battle of wits. In their minds the salesman is a crafty, wily man bent on winning at all costs. The truth is, of course, that this idea is erroneous, out-of-date, unjustified. When a legitimate salesman "wins" a sale there is no loser, for this dominant man is interested in closing sales which benefit the buyer as well as the salesman. It is a point of pride with me that my customers have always gained more from the sales I've closed than I could ever hope to gain. This is as it should be. This is the way I intend to keep closing sales.

Here's a case in point. Kermit Fuller was about to close a sale on a sophisticated piece of machinery to a snack food manufacturer. Kermit knew his equipment. He also was aware that Acme Chip and Snacks, Inc. was losing ground to competition because of obsolescent equipment. But the board of directors was pressuring the firm's president and the plant manager to make out with what they had. They wanted the year's dividends to be fat for the stockholders. Kermit enlisted the help of the president and arranged a meeting with the board of directors. At the meeting, Kermit began with, "Gentlemen, I am here with you to bid the Acme Company goodby forever!"

Kermit let that terrifying thought sink in, then added, "That's not what I want, it's not what your stockholders want, and it's not what you want. Now, I am going to tell you what we must do to prevent that unhappy event."

With that this solid salesman produced factual evidence of what the competition was doing to cut costs and speed production. He also showed in no uncertain manner what was needed to keep Acme viable and profitable.

Over the next two years the whole plant was modernized. Can you guess who the dominant salesman was who closed the sale on every piece of equipment? Further, you can readily sense what a service this man performed for a company that was well on its way to becoming a loser. He more than earned every bit of the $150,000 commission he won by shocking his customer into action.

When you use dominant, authoritative influence to win agreement and close sales, you are on your way to big money. And so are your customers.

PURVES' INSTANT POINTERS ON CLOSING BY PERSONAL DOMINATION

- Domination leaves no doubt in the customer's mind that you are there to close the sale.
- Domination puts you in charge at the closing.
- Domination convinces your customer that the sale should be closed promptly.
- Domination establishes a controlled closing.
- Domination commands attention and smoothes the way for a quick closing.
- Domination makes you a winner by sustaining a high ratio of closed sales to calls.

2

How to Close Under Stiff Competition

When a sale is not closed, what did not happen is as important as what did happen. Often what did not happen was that the salesman involved did not take time to coolly and objectively appraise the competition.

Over the years I have noted that many experienced and dedicated salesmen often attribute supernatural powers and unrealistic deals to the competition. Why this is so I do not know, because, as every successful salesman can tell you, the competition has no secret powers, and often has deals that are not as attractive as the ones you may be able to offer. In fact, it is wise to keep in mind that the competitor sees you in the same awesome light in which you may behold him in an unthinking moment.

Perhaps you have heard the ancient chant that selling is hard work where the law of the jungle still prevails and only the fittest survive. If somebody wished to wax emotional I suppose he could wring his hands and agree unequivocally that it is all true. But, as a viable professional salesman, you know that the statement does not apply to selling any more than it does to accounting, preaching, manufacturing, or any other field of human endeavor. The competition in selling is about of the same force and quality as the competition in any other field of business, or in any other profession. Therefore, when stiff competition looms on the horizon with a big fat super deal, don't panic. Competition is here to stay. That being the case, let's examine some effective ways to deal with it and close sales as we face it.

HOW TO DEBUNK THE "BETTER DEAL"

The biggest favor a hard-working salesman can do the competition is to accept as gospel every rumor and every misconception about the "better deal" the competition has. When you do this you may be handing him an advantage he doesn't really possess. It is not uncommon for a harassed and busy customer, or prospect, to misunderstand the competition's big-hearted offer. Too, in a few cases, a salesman may deliberately be fed misinformation. You don't have to worry as much about this, though, as you do honest misinterpretation. Obviously, the first step in debunking the better deal is to take a good look at it and see what it really is. When you thoroughly understand the "better deal" you are in a much stronger position to start pulling its teeth.

John Motley was whistling happily when he alighted from his car and entered the offices of The Ebbers Company. John had good reason to feel cheerful. He regularly sold Ebbers a number of items, and he always sold at least five hundred cases of a popular beauty product to the account on every trip. Now a customer who can be counted on for a full truck load order on every call is enough to put any salesman in a light-hearted mood. However, after John had written a respectable order he still didn't have his usual five hundred cases of that standard product he was counting on. Of course, he pressed for the order until Ken Murray, the chain's buyer, said, "I'm sorry, John, but I have a better deal."

John was an experienced and aggressive salesman who knew that competition was always barking at his heels. He also knew that he couldn't just lie down and roll over and expect to earn the fat commission he had come to like so well. "Ken," he said, "we have known each other a long time. I just can't understand how anybody could beat the deal I've been able to offer you. Tell me about it."

Ken Murray reached across his desk and handed John the competition's sales brochure. Sure enough, there it was—5% less per case than John's price. But there was one difference. John noticed it at once. The competition was offering a special pack of twenty units to the case. John's firm had the standard twenty-four unit pack. All he had to do to get that lucrative business back was to quietly point out that the competitor's "better deal" was actually costing the customer about 12% more even after the 5% lower price was considered.

Whenever you manage to debunk a "better deal" you reap two readily apparent benefits at once. One, you can close your sale then and there. Two, you add cement to the buyer-seller relationship because you've proven that you are an able, fair, and competent business associate who helps his customer avoid mistakes, and who helps him make extra money. Jim Hodges is a case in point.

Jim was the star salesman for Springfield Paint and Varnish Company, a medium size local manufacturer. Jim's key account was the Commercial and Industrial Paint Contractors, a progressive firm that did large jobs and bought big lots of paint. Suddenly, Jim lost the business. Paint Contractors had a new buyer and he had found a better deal. Or so he thought, until Jim pointed out that his competitor's product had 50% more water in the paint base, and in some cases other fillers. That detracted from the life and the covering qualities of the paint. The Commercial and Industrial Paint Contractors could ill afford to jeopardize their excellent reputation for a few cents less per gallon, Jim reasoned. The new buyer, and Jim's old friends who owned Paint Contractors, agreed. It's been over five years since Jim debunked this "better deal" and he is still closing sale after sale as his customer's business continues to grow.

When the competition comes in with a red hot deal the first thing to do is check it thoroughly. When you know what it really is, how reliable it is, and what makes your customer think that it is so special, then you can marshal your facts and go to work to debunk it. And that is tantamount to closing the sale.

HOW TO CLOSE ON A POINT-BY-POINT COMPARISON

When the competition is rocking your boat you can still close your sale by utilizing a factual point-by-point comparison. Any competitor is bound to have a weak spot. This exacting comparison can uncover it for you, and for your customer. When you've found it, that is the time to close your sale. Here's how:

You cannot deal in generalities when closing a sale on a point-by-point basis. The areas where you or your product excel must be clearly and specifically delineated. It is not enough to say "My product is better than his product," "My product performs better than his product," "My product lasts longer than his product," or "I will take better care of you than he will."

No, the generalities are too weak to be convincing. And only conviction leads to the closed sale. You must explain *why* and *how* your product is superior to the competitor's; you must explain *why* and *how* your product performs better; you must explain *why* and *how* your product will last longer than the competitor's. Of course, you will be obliged to explain how you can take better care of your customer than anybody else can. As you close in this manner you can, point-by-point, show the extra benefits and advantages you are able to provide the customer. No matter how long you may have known the man, or how fond he may be of you, he still wants to know what is in it for him. This is the only sound reason he will have to help you close the sale and refuse the aggressive competition a slice of the pie. It is the salesman's job to furnish the proof. When you face up to this obligation you have every right to close the sale.

A good pen will help you close your sale on a point-by-point basis. When you put your strategy in writing you avoid deadly generalities and concentrate on key issues. That will close your sale.

Here's an example of how Tom Fairlee put his point-by-point comparison on paper when a competitor had about convinced his client to buy a cheaper life insurance policy.

POINTS

Annual Premium:	competitor—$850.00
	My proposal—$1000.00
Amount of Insurance:	Competitor—$40,000
	My proposal—$40,000
Cash Values:	Competitor—None for first 10 years
	My proposal—*Cash values start building the first year.
	*(Show company schedule)
Assets of Respective Corporations:	Competitor—$7,000,000
	Mine—$11,000,000,000
Length of time in business:	Competitor—3 years
	My company—101 years
Claims paying record:	Competitor—So far, so good, but no long-term trend established yet.
	My company—Prompt and in full for 101 years.
Dividends:	Competitor—None of record
	My company—Paid every three months for 100 years.
Advantages to my customer of my proposal	(1) Less net cost.
	(2) Trustworthy savings program as cash values accumulate.

POINTS

(3) **Expert agent and agency to service account.**
(4) **Security of strong, proven company.**
(5) **Strategically located national claim offices.**
(6) **Strong financial position of my company guarantees protection for client's family and business.**

Tom uses a legal pad to do his written work, but that is merely a matter of personal preference. It's not the paper that closes the sale. It's what you put on it, and how strongly you present it. You can vary Tom's method to suit your own particular product. A good pen will close sales for you under stiff competition just as it does for Tom Fairlee.

HOW TO DRAMATIZE YOUR DEPENDABILITY

As every intelligent marketing man knows, not every competitor is a rank amateur or a blatant fool. The experienced salesman knows that he can expect to run into situations where the competitor is offering goods or services that compare favorably in many ways to his own. In this case, while still probing for the competition's weak spots, you must "dramatize" the extras your own personality will bring to the customer.

One of the most important things a customer-buyer looks for in a salesman is dependability. In other words, he wants yours to be a dependable personality—one that he can count on day in and day out as he struggles to keep ahead of his own competition. When the competition stiffens its back and tries to bring its goods and services in line with yours, it is then high time for you to dramatize your dependability. *Dependability* is a potent tool that can close sales under fire.

As a Chicago salesman once told me, if you have been calling on a customer long enough for him to know that you are conscientious and dependable, then you can dramatize your track record. But if your history isn't all that lengthy you can still dramatize your dependability to help you close your sale. Here are some effective ideas that have been used to establish a salesman's dependability and to give him the edge to close despite frenetic pressure from the competition.

Use showmanship to plant in your customer's mind the importance of your dependability. Blow up the specter of troubles that might arise in dealing with a less than dependable salesman. Stress your own conviction that dependability is worth time and money to him as well as to you. Ask for the opportunity to demonstrate the worth of your responsible performance to him. Explain that it can all begin as soon as you have closed the sale at stake. When he agrees, deliver dependability along with the goods, so that you will see more than a closed door on return trips.

Of course, a long period of service on the job and in the territory can always be cited as evidence of trustworthy dependability. The customer will usually accept an extended record in the field as sufficient assurance that you are a man of your word. He will then feel comfortable as you close your sale. Take full advantage of this plus if it is yours.

Most salesmen keep a customer file or diary of some sort. Such a file can be used as Exhibit A to dramatize your dependability.

The file I maintain is invaluable to me. It is also simple. I have a small metal box large enough to hold two or three hundred 3 × 5 index cards. I prefer the ruled cards. On each card is the customer's name, exact name of his business, address, phone number, bank, credit references, potential, and best hours to call. Too, I leave room to make notes of anything new and exciting, such as an award he has earned, a trip he has planned, a new baby, etc. I want to be able to show any genuine interest by recalling such incidents on my return trip. Of course, I'm careful to record my sales to him. Also, I'm careful to make a note on anything he expressed an interest in, so that I'll have this ammo to help close the next sale. Here's an example of what goes on my little 3 × 5 customer cards.

> **Sunflower Carpet and Flooring. Owner: Joe Nesbitt**
> **(wife Charlene).**
> **222 Pacific Avenue**
> **Big City, Kansas 67156**
> **Phone:Bus. 816-432-9111. Home, 816-432-8763**
> **Carrier: Big Moss Truck Lines**
> **5/23—Sold 5 rolls Starfire with free decorator**
> **boards for store and salesmen.**
> **(Next trip: says he will stock new style Starbright)**

On the back of the card will be listed his bank, trade references, and business potential.

I think so much of these little evidences of dependability that I'm reluctant to leave them in my car. I take them right into the motel room with me at night. I want to have them handy to dramatize my dependability the next day.

Of course, references from your other customers can help establish your dependability. The best way to do this is to select a few that your buyer can call at once. Be sure that *you* pay for the calls.

Your company's policy concerning dependable performance should be a matter of record. Don't hesitate to use it. A dependable firm and a dependable salesman are hard to beat when it comes to closing sales the competition is after.

Your dependability is your own potent sales tool. Dramatize it when you need extra power to close a sale your competitor is trying to grab from you. Employ the ideas discussed, as well as any others that you may find, to enhance your posture as a loyal, dependable salesman whose business it is to close sales.

BE THERE FIRST

When competition is baying at your heels like a pack of hungry wolves, getting to the customer first can eliminate a lot of problems. Obviously, if you close the sale before your competitor gets to your customer, he won't have much to bark at but the moon. When you're in the field, keep your eyes and ears open. It's much easier to close the sale if you get there first.

BEWARE INDIRECT COMPETITION

The other ambitious salesman isn't the only competitor out to keep you from closing a sale. The indirect competition that keeps you sidetracked can be as rough as a roaring competitor with a toothy smile and a big sample case.

Here are a few sources of indirect competition:

- Too much socializing on the job.
- Quitting early or starting late so that you can catch a favorite TV program.
- Staying up so late that you're too tired to fight the next morning.
- Doing paper work during selling hours.
- Worrying overmuch about what the competitor has to sell. (Why should you do this? You don't have his lines. Let him worry about what he has to sell. Expend your energies closing sales on your lines.)

- Any other time-consuming item that is not pitched directly at closing the sale promptly.

Sometimes it takes more will power to deal with the indirect competition than it does to deal with the more apparent kind. Better organizing and planning, with a bit of determination, can whip this insidious competition so that you can use otherwise wasted time to close more sales.

HOW TO USE THE COMPETITION TO FORCE A CLOSING

The first time I heard someone say that he had used competition to force a buying decision, I felt sure that he had gone off his rocker. It happened at a Rochester sales meeting years ago. When I raised my eyebrows, Pat Iverson offered to show me how as soon as we went home to our adjoining territories. I had to respect Pat's seniority, but I still wanted to see how he did it. The next Monday morning I met Pat at a nearby town and watched him do just what he had promised.

Pat sold a franchised line to wholesalers. He had been getting encouragement and little else from the biggest wholesaler in the area. Now a competitor to Pat with a similar line had moved into the area. Both Pat and Gordon Barker of Barker Wholesale and Supply knew this.

Pat had arranged a 9 a.m. appointment. After introductions this is what I saw and heard:

Pat: "Mr. Barker, you know what I have to offer you and, no doubt, you know the details of ARCO Company's deal. I think you will agree that what I have to offer in merchandise, service, and advertising is the best in the business. Isn't that right?"

Barker: "Yes."

Pat: "Mr. Barker, I'm obliged to insist on a decision from you today. There are two distributors in the area and my competitor is going to get one of them sooner or later. But I'm going to be affiliated with one of them today. As you know, you are my first choice. I don't think that we should delay another day. You need the business and so do I. Together we can pretty well control it in the area. It would be a pleasure to work with you, and I hope you agree that now is the time to get started."

Barker: "You're coming on pretty strong, Mr. Iverson! But I don't want my competitor to have your line."

Pat: "Thank you, Mr. Barker. And I certainly don't want my competitor to have your business."

Barker: "I'm tied up until about two o'clock. Why don't you write a tentative opening order and come in then. I'll have my buyer give you the purchase order, and I want you to go over the line and your promotion schedule with him."

That was it. It may not always be that simple, but you can frequently use competition to force a closing when all else has failed.

Another approach that's been employed to close an impressive sale is this:

A midwest salesman had been trying to close a sale for a packaging machine with a buyer who didn't like to be "bothered." On the second call this salesman put the competition to work to close his sale by saying, "Mr. Craig, you've told me you don't like to be bothered. I can appreciate that. However, you know that my competition is going to be after you until you have made a choice right or wrong. I know that you cannot do as well with anyone else as you can with me. That's what you told me last week. So let's close this deal today. Then you can put the equipment to work and enjoy your usual peace of mind."

You know your product, your line, your policies, better than anybody else. You know, or should know, your competition better than anybody else. Watch for the competition's blunders and weak spots. Then, when the competition gets stiff, you can turn the tables and use the competition to force a closing.

PURVES' INSTANT POINTERS ON CLOSING SALES UNDER STIFF COMPETITION

- Don't make a superman of the competitor.
- Debunk the competition's "better deal" with facts and figures and close your sale with proof.
- You can eliminate the competition and close your sales with a convincing point-by-point comparison.
- Getting there first makes it easier to close the sale.
- Don't let the unseen enemy "indirect competition" keep you from closing your sale.
- You can analyze the competition and develop strategy to put your competition to work to close your sale.
- You benefit from competition because:
  A. It keeps you alert and on fire to close the sale.
  B. It can make you look good to your customer as you skillfully handle it.
  C. It affords you the opportunity to prove your right to the closed sale.

3

How to Put Product Knowledge to Work to Close Your Deal

Before you decide that this topic is too elementary for you, read on! The cost of training a salesman is enormous both in money and time. The pressure to put a man in the field and producing is great. The salesman himself is anxious to get on with it. Commendably, he wants to make money, to prove himself. The upshot of all this is that zeal may be prodigious, but product knowledge may suffer. Don't let this happen to you. As every money-making, enthusiastic, experienced salesman knows, it's fatal to slight the basics in this profession.

PRODUCT KNOWLEDGE IS BASIC

Product knowledge is basic to closing a sale. Your customer may like your personality, he may have the utmost regard for your firm, but when he buys a product from you he expects you to be the final authority on that product. Before he closes a deal with you, he wants your assurance that your product will meet his expectations. Further, if any problems develop he will be looking for your expertise to get him out of his difficulty. This is all a very real part of closing any sale whether the product be tangible or intangible.

Product knowledge is basic enough that few buyers will tolerate a salesman who is so ill prepared that he cannot intelligently present his case. In fact, in the fast-paced markets of today the salesman who fails to prepare himself adequately in this area cannot expect to command attention or respect. Closing a sale without these two ingredients (attention and respect) is unimaginable. With basic product knowledge you command the attention and respect that paves the way to the closed sale.

Since product knowledge is obviously fundamental in closing the sale, the sales leaders in any field are constantly studying and working to learn every scrap of information about their product. They know that it is vital to be aware of every benefit it may offer the customer or prospect. And while every leading manufacturer or firm will go to great lengths to impart product knowledge, the ambitious, creative salesman must use his own time and initiative to learn even more about his product. There are multiple ready sources for additional product knowledge over and beyond your sales manuals. Among these are more experienced men, helpful customers, knowledgeable sales executives, trade journals, and the technical people who develop and improve the products you sell. The better prepared you are in the basics of product knowledge, the better prepared you are to close more than your share of sales. And this is where the money gets big.

HOW TO USE PRODUCT KNOWLEDGE
TO CLOSE YOUR SALE ON THE SPOT

Product knowledge is the built-in advantage in closing a sale on the spot. For example, Ron Daniels, a beginner in the industrial sales field, had gained an audience with the purchasing agent of a company that required much steel tubing. The first question tossed to Ron was, "How often do you cycle your production?"

Now, Ron had a catalog of sizes and gauges, along with prices, but nobody had told him about "production cycles." So he hesitated, then offered the buyer his catalog to examine while he went back to check on "cycles." Just as he left, and while the P.A. still stood there with Ron's catalog, another salesman with tubing on his mind came through the door.

The P.A. played no favorites. He asked the same question of this salesman. The difference was that this salesman had the product knowledge right then and there. He declared to the P.A. that his firm cycled production every three weeks and possibly could do better in an emergency. Further, he explained that sizes 6 to 16 inches were readily available in eight gauges. He emphasized that his firm was flexible and would cut to any length and provide any desired end treatment.

When Ron returned he learned a hard lesson. The other salesman had the order and was already anticipating the fat $2000 commission his product knowledge had earned for him.

Basic product knowledge will close sales on the spot. You don't have to learn that the hard way as Ron did.

HOW TO USE PRODUCT KNOWLEDGE ON CALLBACKS

The best of salesmen must sometimes try more than once in order to close a rewarding sale. External circumstances can intrude, the salesman may have omitted a crucial point under the pressure of time, the buyer may have had a stomach ache, or one of a thousand outside influences could have fouled the first sales interview. Or the salesman could have omitted one important bit of product knowledge. In such cases, the experienced man knows he must go back and finish the job or leave it for someone else to reap the fat commission. That is an agonizing prospect to any conscientious salesman. Few pros can idly entertain the thought.

A thorough and keen product knowledge is, as we know, a great asset in closing any sale. It is vitally essential when it is necessary to make a callback to close a sale. A review of what happened is in order when the sale was not closed on the original call. Here are some areas to double check as you prepare to use your expert's product knowledge to go back and close your sale.

- Did I have the customer's undivided attention as I explained the product?
- Did I re-emphasize the features that appealed to him most?
- Did I specify the benefits especially applicable to my customer's needs?
- Did I speak unhesitatingly and with confidence about my product's features?
- Were there items relating to product knowledge (such as a planned national promotional campaign) which I failed to push vigorously?
- What sales features might I have overlooked the first time I attempted to close with product knowledge?

James Curnutt, who sells wall coverings, had to go back before he closed a sale that netted him $1750 in commissions. He had called on a contractor responsible for the installation of acoustical wall coverings in a new office complex. The contractor had agreed that Curnutt's fabric was attractive, functional, had excellent sound absorption qualities, would be easy to maintain, and was allergy free. Further, price was no problem. It seemed to have everything, but Mr. Curnutt had not closed his sale on the first go round. After intense reflection and many notes on what had and had not transpired, salesman Curnutt realized he had failed to show that his product had the architect's approval. Back Mr. Curnutt went to correct this oversight. He did a thorough job and nailed down the closed sale by intensifying his use of product knowledge, and by pushing a bit of key related product knowledge, to close his sale on the callback.

When you recheck every feature with searching concentration you are in an excellent position to put your product knowledge to use to close your sale on any necessary re-runs. Mr. Curnutt's example points out how one product feature can put your commission in your pocket as you go back to use product knowledge on a callback.

HOW TO USE PRODUCT KNOWLEDGE TO KNOCK OUT PUT-OFFS

Every salesman must deal with put-offs. The only exception might be a hesitant salesman pussyfooting around the tough boys — and thereby missing a lot of lucrative business. But that is not for a dynamic salesman out to close every sale possible. When you run into a put-off you can knock it out with expert product knowledge. Here's how the pros do it:

Paul Hite, salesman for a huge restaurant supply firm, was on the verge of closing a sale for a twin drink dispenser for each unit of a franchise chain group. But the spokesman for the buying committee kept stalling because, as he said, he had to be sure the unit could be quickly and easily cleaned. Too, he insisted that the machine's refrigeration system had to speedily chill the warm juice drink when it was necessary to refill the bowl. Paul was ready. The manufacturer was well-known and reliable, he pointed out. Then he laid the specifications of the drink dispenser on the table for all three members of the buying committee to see. All agreed the machine met the desired criteria with the added value of extra cooling capacity. Paul had already obtained price approval, and when he affirmed he could effect delivery within two weeks — well ahead of the chain's peak season — the sale was closed. As a clincher, Paul arranged for his company's service man to make a pilot installation with the chain's service man so that no store manager would be without ready assistance. The initial order was for seventy-five twin dispensers on which Paul won a ten dollar PM for each machine placed, as well as his usual commission. Product knowledge knocked out this put-off and paid the salesman $2250 when he closed his sale.

When your product knowledge is razor sharp you can establish how your customer can benefit at once from your proposition. When you do that you are in an excellent position to knock out any put-offs and close your sale then and there.

PRODUCT KNOWLEDGE GIVES YOU
THE AUTHORITY TO CLOSE

Product knowledge makes an authority of you. With this knowledge you have valid authority to close your sale. The most important thing you can do is to be sure you use your product knowledge in such a manner that your customer easily understands what you are saying. Too, since technical lingo may confuse your buyer, use enough of your product knowledge to wrap up your sale, then stop.

I witnessed a sad little drama one day while sitting in the office of a friend of mine. Olin Paschall is the housewares buyer for a large discount department store. On this particular day Olin was keeping two appointments before we went to lunch. Both salesmen sold, among other things, crock cookers. This was the item Olin was considering.

The first man came in and showed Olin a nice unit. He spoke glowingly and enthusiastically. He mentioned a few key features of his crock cooker, but what he really spent his time on was the vast technical resources of his company, the long and extensive history of his firm, and the exacting course he had gone through to learn about crock cookery. After about fifteen minutes Olin glanced at his watch, explained that he had another appointment, and thanked the salesman for the descriptive literature he had handed Olin.

Now, the other salesman appeared to keep his appointment. He brought in a crock cooker, sat it in front of Olin, and pointed out these features quickly:

- 4 ½ quart capacity.
- The outside of the unit would always remain cool.
- Required small storage space. Size was only 8″ × 13″ × 10″.
- Had a detachable cord so that leftover food could be stored and refrigerated right in the cooking pot.
- The pot was easy and convenient to use as a serving dish.
- An excellent recipe book was packed with each pot at no additional cost.
- The unit required a minimum of energy.
- The manufacturer had a supporting national advertising program.

* The salesman's company could and would effect prompt delivery.

Of course, the second salesman closed the sale. He had full authority to do so, because he furnished Olin with the product information that he needed to make a favorable buying decision. No doubt salesman number one was just as educated and just as earnest as salesman number two. But number two established his authority to close by putting his product knowledge up front to close the sale without embroidery.

Your product knowledge gives you the authority to close your sale. With this potent authority you can close your deal in a minimum of time and move on to the next profitable business transaction.

HOW TO USE PRODUCT KNOWLEDGE TO CLOSE AS PLANNED

It is just as important to plan how to close your sale as it is to plan who you are going to see and when and where you are going to see him. In fact, unless you have a well-defined, strong plan to close your sale, all your other planning may very well turn out to be nothing more than an exercise in futility. Product knowledge is a powerful closing tool. You can use it to close as planned. Here's how:

Planning on paper is more reliable and effective than making a few little mental notes for the morrow as you prepare for bed. Planning on paper need not be an onerous task. It can and should be quick, brief, and to the point. Planning is for your personal benefit and use. No frills are necessary.

Here's a good way to chart your product knowledge so that you will overlook nothing as you close per your plan. Let us say that you are planning to sell a big stocking order of floor polishing to a giant home care center. List on one side of a sheet of paper every selling advantage your product offers. On the other side list what benefits your dealer will realize.

Product: Super-Keen Floor Polish

Selling Advantages	Dealer Benefits
• Good gloss.	• Easy to display.
• Scuff resistant.	• Easy to sell because of the positive advantages.
• Wear resistant.	
• Skid resistant.	• Good profit margin.

Selling Advantages	Dealer Benefits
• Water spotting resistant.	• Quick turnover.
• Freedom from haze.	• Quantity discounts.
• Has touch-up ability.	• Opening order bonus.
• Competitively priced.	• Co-op advertising program.
• Easy application.	

No matter whether you are selling mutual funds or industrial boilers, you can use this same technique to consolidate your product knowledge in order to close your sale as planned. The more selling advantages, and the more benefits you list, the more authority you will have to close as you planned to close. You may not need to use every item on your list, but it's helpful to have back-up reserves when needed. A closed sale is too important to omit any product knowledge which can help get it on the order book as planned.

PURVES' INSTANT POINTERS ON PUTTING PRODUCT KNOWLEDGE TO WORK TO CLOSE YOUR DEAL

- Product knowledge is the basic built-in advantage in closing your deal.
- Product knowledge is basic to closing because buyers cannot deal solely with personalities.
- Product knowledge can knock out put-offs and close your sale on the spot.
- Product knowledge gives you the authority to close.
- Product knowledge eliminates wasted motion and wasted time by enabling you to close as planned.
- Product knowledge is money knowledge.

4

How to Close in the Face of Price Objections

Price objections may terrify the novice when he tries to close his sale, but, as any seasoned pro knows, sales are routinely closed in the face of strenuous price objections every day. It is the norm, for price objections are part of the buyer's natural resistance. Price objections are used to probe for a better deal, to discourage weak salesmen, and to satisfy the buyer that he is buying at the most advantageous price. I learned long ago that price objections are not a signal that the interview is over and the sale lost forever. No, it is not that. Rather, it is a wide open buying signal.

Here's a little self-administered test. Take a large sheet of clean white paper, the bigger the better. Carefully paint or color a small black dot exactly in the center of the big white sheet of paper. Let the black dot represent price objections. The white unblemished area represents the selling features of your product — the features that will close your sale for you. Lean the big sheet of paper with the little black dot against the wall or hang it on the wall. Step back across the room from it. What do you see?

Of course, what you see and what holds your attention is the black dot — the price objection. Yet there is much, much more of the snowy white area — your selling features.

Make this test. It will help you keep price objection in perspective as you close your sale.

PRICE OBJECTIONS:
AN OPEN INVITATION TO CLOSE

When a customer or prospect voices price objections he is, in truth, expressing a keen interest in what you have to sell. If he had absolutely no interest in your product he would not care one way or the other what your price might be. Assuredly, he would not trouble you about it if he were not hoping to do business with you — business on his terms, perhaps, but business. It follows then, that at this point your work is cut out for you. You must justify your price by spelling out the benefits you and your product can offer the customer. This is what he is really asking you to do when he complains that your price is too high. He is not slamming the door in your face. Instead, he is extending to you an open invitation to close your sale.

THE PRICE BUYER IS VULNERABLE

Tough as he may sound at times, the price buyer is vulnerable. Of course, he may be taken in occasionally by succumbing to a price so ridiculously low that he gets much less than he bargained for. But that is not what we mean when we say that the price buyer is vulnerable. The price buyer is vulnerable to logic and good sense. He knows that a price is low only in relation to the value he receives. It is your job to prove to him that he is getting more value than price alone. This is not an impossible task when you know how to close under price intimidation.

HOW TO HANDLE "PRICE INTIMIDATION"

As any career-minded professional salesman can attest, there are still a few well-intentioned buyers around who operate on the theory that bullying the salesman is the way to win price concessions. Unfortunately, this tactic apparently does work once in a while when a too-eager salesman panics and gives away his rightful commission and compromises his company's profits. Rash price concessions are not only questionable, they may be downright unlawful. The law states that special prices must be justified and may be granted only under specified conditions. Intimidation is not one of these conditions. As a strong and skillful salesman, you will not succumb to the bullying tactics of price intimidation for any reason. There are tested methods to handle this problem and close your sale. For instance:

Earl Curtis sat across the desk from Scott Ellwood. Mr. Ellwood was head of the purchasing department for Home Center Enterprises, Incorporated, a chain consisting of ten supermarket type building supply centers. Earl had quoted a price on a truck load of windows for each of Home Center Enterprises' stores. As you can surmise a sizable commission was at stake. To be exact: $5610.00 in commissions was hanging in limbo as Mr. Ellwood was belligerently saying, "Earl, you know blankety-blank well that we are your biggest account. You'll have to shave that price if you want our business!"

Now, Earl had been subjected to that unrelenting pressure for at least fifteen painful minutes. At this point he arose, picked up his proposal, and said, "Mr. Ellwood, you know that I want your business, but, as I've explained, that is the best price I can offer. I'm aware that I'm not the only one with windows for sale, but I know the price I've been authorized to quote to you is more than fair. Thank you for giving me the opportunity to quote." And with that he left.

Two days later Earl had a phone call. Mr. Ellwood had reconsidered. Earl lost no time in getting back to Mr. Ellwood's office. The meeting was cordial. Earl left not only with his closed sale for windows, but also two truck loads of doors had been added to the original order.

Standing your ground in the face of price intimidation is good business. This way you can close profitable, meaningful sales, as Earl's case illustrates.

Buyers who employ price intimidation are using old and crude tactics. However, they do not often completely abandon reason. Keep this in mind and you can close your sale on equitable terms. Both you and your customer win when your sale is closed in the light of sweet reason despite price intimidation.

HOW TO USE VALUE TO CLOSE

No doubt there are times in the life of every hard-working salesman when he feels that prices are the only thing a customer ever thinks about. Yet we all know that price is not the only consideration. Indeed, despite the bluster and thunder so often associated with price, it is seldom the main consideration. *Value* will close more sales than price alone. When the salesman is equipped (as he always should be) to present the *value* of his product or proposition, he is in an enviable position to close his sale.

For an example, let us take an item as uncomplicated as a common hand-operated bicycle pump and see how value (you may substitute "quality" for the word "value" if you wish) may be used to close a sale.

BRAND XX BICYCLE PUMP

Price: $8.00
Features:
  Height — 19″
  Hose — 19″ — unreinforced
  Handle — uncomfortable — two nuts
  that could work loose.

BRAND AA BICYCLE PUMP

Price: $12.00
Features:
  Height — 26½″
  Small bore for easy pumping
  Handle — large, easy grip
  Hose — 25½″ — reinforced for added efficiency

Now let's look at the value in Brand AA that represents closing points over and beyond the 50% price differential.

Height:	A comfortable 26½″ as compared to the 19″ height of brand XX which is too low for comfort.
Hose:	26½″ to reach tire valve easily. The 19″ length of brand XX won't reach the valve if the tire is not positioned. Too, the 19″ is not reinforced.
Handle:	Large and comfortable. Brand XX handle is small and poorly secured.
Also:	Brand AA has the added value of a small hose for easy pumping.

Let me ask you: If you were selling bicycle pumps for a living would you rather have the $8.00 price of Brand XX or the added value of the $12.00 brand AA to help close your sales?

I'm sure you will agree that you could use the value of Brand AA to close a great many more sales than you could ever hope to close by relying on the shoddier product with the lower price. Value is always a stronger closing tool than the over-rated low price factor. Value represents benefits, and benefits close sales.

HOW TO USE VALUE TO WHIP THE LOW PRICE FACTOR AND CLOSE YOUR SALE

Frank Newman had to overcome the low price factor in order to close a floor covering sale for $89,520 to a builder of high rise apartments. Mrs. Lynn Gilder, the builder's wife, was in charge of decorating. She also had the responsibility of buying all the materials she used. The project at hand involved a purchase of 7460 square yards of carpet. Mrs. Gilder had selected the style and color she wanted, and Frank had been able to quote a price of twelve dollars per square yard. "Too high!" the lady screamed.

Frank knew his price represented real value. He also knew Mrs. Gilder was a housewife, and he was prepared to use value to close.

This thinking salesman reached into his brief case and pulled a twelve inch square wash cloth from his bag. He spread the wash cloth on Mr. Gilder's desk and asked, "How much would you expect to pay for a wash cloth like this, Mrs. Gilder?"

Mrs. Gilder replied, "I don't know why you ask, but I would say about two dollars."

"You're close," Frank answered, "and would you say $1.95 would be a real value?"

"Yes, I would," said Mrs. Gilder.

Now Frank threw in his clincher as he used value to whip the low price factor and close his sale. "Mrs. Gilder," Frank explained, "at $1.95, which is what I paid for this wash cloth, it would cost $17.55 to buy one square yard of this material. In view of this, don't you agree that the product, plus the wearability and other benefits you have recognized in my carpet, is a superior value for only twelve dollars per square yard?"

Mrs. Gilder smiled and said, "Frank, you've got me!"

When your customer vocally objects to your price he is saying in effect, "What's in it for me? What am I getting that makes your product, or service, more valuable to me than the money I must part with in order to own it?"

This is a fair question. It is a question which the professional salesman anticipates, and one that he is prepared to answer. When you answer this question you can whip the low price factor and close your sale just as Frank Newman did. Incidentally, Frank's commission on his sale was $4475—not all the money in the world, but a good day's pay.

THERE'S MORE TO CLOSING THE SALE
THAN QUOTING THE PRICE

When you must close your sale in the face of vicious price objections, remember this: There's more to closing the sale than quoting the price.

Art Sconneli sells canoes and river boats to RV centers and marine dealers. He had just been told by Pete Cummins of Table Rock Outfitters that the price on his new inflatable boat was "too high." Art had already detailed how his boat was constructed of 26 gauge heavy duty Poly Vinyl Cloride, had a tight seal design, safety air valves, and a one year guarantee. Now he pulled out his reserves to add more logic and good sense to his presentation. His price buyer was vulnerable. Art again pointed out that families comprised most of the dealer's business. Then he showed that his boat was actually a two-in-one boat because it had inner air chambers as well as outer air chambers. If one chamber developed a leak the boat would still float until the family could make it to shore. This feature of independent air chambers was a great sales feature to families with small children. The dealer didn't have to be reminded again who his prime customers were. He gave Art an order for fifteen on the spot. Before the summer was gone he sold eighty-nine. No big deal, says Art, but $1980 that he wouldn't have earned otherwise.

Your price buyer is just as vulnerable as Art's. And the commissions are equally as juicy.

Shatterproof glass costs more than ordinary glass and rightly so. George Drago who is a sales leader and top money man for Home and Car Glass Company knows this. To his credit as an experienced pro, George also has a penetrating appreciation of the fact that there is more to closing the sale than merely quoting the price. He is always prepared to utilize this insight when he is closing a sale. As George encounters the bugaboo of price resistance he has his customer make a test. He does this by handing the customer, or prospect, a small hammer and two pieces of glass from a sales kit that he carries for such occasions. One piece of glass is plain glass; the other is Shatterproof, or "Safety" glass. George asks the customer to use the hammer and break each piece of glass. Of course, the ordinary glass breaks easily and flies into fragments with sharp and dangerous cutting edges. The shatterproof glass is hard to break and the fragments are not the sharp hazards that the plain glass fragments are. This proof positive justifies George's price. It also closes many sales for him as his track record will attest.

It would be a sorry situation for business, and for mankind, if the only way a sale could be closed was on the basis of low price. The world's merchandise would deteriorate to the lowest common denominator. Commerce would fall into ill repute and utter disarray, while the intelligence and energies of vibrant marketing men would seek more challenging fields. If the lowest price should ever be the one and only consideration in closing sales, our standard of living would fall disastrously. The whole fabric of life as we know it would suffer.

All this places an awesome responsibility on the active salesman. He must close his sales on values and benefits rather than price alone. This is how you discharge your obligation to your industry, your profession, and your customer. This is how you close profitable, worthwhile sales in the face of price objections.

PURVES' INSTANT POINTERS ON HOW TO CLOSE IN THE FACE OF PRICE OBJECTIONS

- Recognize price objections as buying signals.
- Price objections are an open invitation to close.
- The price buyer is vulnerable.
- Buyers who practice "price intimidation" are responsive to logic and reason.
- You can whip the low price factor with a skillful use of *value*.
- *Value* and *benefits* outrank *price* as sales closing techniques.
- There's more to closing the sale than quoting the price.

5

How to Use Demonstrations to Close

SAMPLES PLUS IMAGINATION = DYNAMITE!

Samples are among a salesman's hottest selling tools. They have only one serious handicap — they do not have a real, live, vivid imagination to flash on when needed to close a sale. This all to the good, because this affords you the opportunity to be creative, to inject your own personality and imagination into the selling procedure. And, as any experienced, powerful salesman will tell you, a vibrant, warm personality and an exciting imagination can melt resistance and close sales. Simply put, samples plus imagination = dynamite!

I've heard earnest salesmen complain, "But I don't have an imagination!" If you should share this unfortunate view, remember this: imagination is not magic. You don't have to be a wizard to develop a bit of work-a-day imagination. You merely use your mind (imagination) to demonstrate the uses and benefits of what you are selling. Then you focus it all on the closing of your sale as you demonstrate what you say with samples.

To stimulate your imagination and more effectively use your samples to close, you can watch the man on television. The ad agencies' stock in trade is imagination. You can adapt their imaginative ideas to close your own sales as you watch the television actors and models demonstrate the better razor, the incredible flashlight batteries, the gorgeous new models of color TV sets, the alluring perfumes and soaps, the amazing household detergents, and on and on.

It doesn't take much to visualize the truth of this: You must show and demonstrate your samples with imagination in order to close your sale. It is not enough to merely let your customer *look* at them.

Stewart Amber works the hardware and home center trade with a line of adhesives and sealants. One of his faster moving products is a silicone rubber sealant. Stewart says it will work wonders around the home and shop. He carries samples and uses his imagination to prove his point and close his sale. He always has a tube of sealant handy along with pieces of wood, glass, leather, plastic and metal. He uses his samples with a flair as he shows how his product will perform. He glues together two dissimilar materials, for example, as well as gluing similar materials. He also repairs cracks and breaks in some of the items he has brought in to use with his sample. As he makes these quick, convincing demonstrations he holds up his sample and explains how it can be used to fill crevices around bathtubs, sinks, windshields, and foundations. He also tells how it can repair broken toys, ponchos, refrigerators, and ovens. By this time the pieces he has glued together with his sealant have set, so he has his customer try to pull them apart. Of course, the sample has done its job and Stewart closes his sale at this point.

Stewart knows that samples plus imagination = dynamite! For the last five years he has won an all-expenses paid trip for two to some exciting far-away spot. Incidentally, he also earns a healthy income and is easily his firm's leading salesman. Stewart says samples and imaginative demonstrations will close sales for any determined salesman. I, for one, believe him. Samples plus imagination = dynamite!

DON'T DECIDE AHEAD OF TIME
WHAT THE CUSTOMER WON'T LIKE

Most salesmen have more than one item to offer. Often each item will be in different styles, colors, sizes, flavors, gauges, assortments, etc. It is work to take in a lot of samples. It is a costly mistake not to do so. Whatever you do, don't decide ahead of time what the customer won't like. The sample you leave outside in your car cannot help you close your sale.

In this matter of deciding ahead of time what the customer won't — or will — like, consider this: If this were feasible, manufacturers would curtail their production to only what their customers already liked, incentive would lessen, new products and ideas would diminish, samples would be few, and salesmen would be relegated to the unglamorous and ill-paying role of order takers. Happily, though, the pulsating markets of today abound with an exhilarating variety of goods. In the same tone and sense, today's marketing men appreciate the opportunity that such a catalog of goods and samples gives them. They don't decide what the customer won't like ahead of time. They sample and demonstrate and close more sales than ever before.

My old friend, Pop Jaynes, who sold drugs for one of the world's biggest drug houses until he was more than eighty years old, continued to rely on samples and demonstrations to close sales right up until his last sales call. Pop became so frail and enfeebled that his wife drove for him towards the end of his career. She would sometimes chide the old fellow for carrying in his samples and making demonstrations on each call. She felt he was so well-known and liked that this was no longer necessary. Pop would only smile and remind her that no salesman ever lived long enough, or was so loved, that samples and demonstrations wouldn't help him close more sales.

As you've surmised, Pop spoke from heartfelt conviction. He had long since passed the time in his life when he worked from sheer necessity. Yet he still refused to fall into the trap of deciding ahead of time what his customer wouldn't like.

HOW TO USE SAMPLES TO CLOSE BY COMPARISON

Unless you are the only salesman in the world there will be times when you must close your sale on the basis of a one-on-one comparison. When this happens (as it will), the most effective way to close your sale is through a solid demonstration employing samples. There are a number of key points to keep in mind as you demonstrate your product under the stress of a one-on-one comparison. It is not necessary to discuss these in order of their importance. Your own individual sales situation will dictate which is more important to you at the time.

First, you should always handle your samples with respect as you make a sales demonstration. If you give the customer the impression that you do not regard them highly he can't be expected to attach much importance to your samples or to your demonstration. And poof! there goes your closed sale.

Housewares and jewelry salesmen know the necessity of treating samples with loving care. They wrap them carefully and keep them spotless and shiny for each demonstration. I've even heard of a plumbing salesman who keeps his samples wrapped in velvet and carefully unwraps and polishes each piece as he shows it to his dealers. I personally make it a point to keep my samples looking good. I take care of them and demonstrate them with pride. This is the only way to do it if you expect to close that sale — especially if you're making a one-on-one comparison against a rip-roaring competitor who would love to close the sale for you.

One more thought before we get away from this matter of treating your samples with respect and pride: You know that you can't go in and spread your samples before your customer and say "Help yourself!" You must be ready with a planned, organized, and rehearsed demonstration. Your samples will close sales for you, but you must give them dignity and voice to get the job done.

Second, a good idea when your demonstration is going to be made against another product is to be sure you know what you are up against. Don't go in blindfolded. In a demonstration involving a comparison it is mandatory that you know where and how your product is superior. This is what you must be prepared to demonstrate in order to close your sale.

It is important, too, to have the individual attention of your customer when you are using samples in your demonstration. Don't waste your time or your samples by trying to demonstrate your goods to someone who is hopscotching all over the place, or trying to listen to half a dozen other people at the same time. Tactfully explain that his attention is necessary and expected. If your customer can't comply with this reasonable and polite request, arrange another time when he can listen to you. Then go out the door and on to another call where the odds against your closing your sale are not so staggering.

I know a lot of floor covering salesmen. Ovis McIntyre is one of the better ones. Here's how I saw him win a truck load carpet order by using his samples to close by comparison. Ovis sells to wholesale distributors only. These wholesalers are, of necessity, mighty price conscious. But they also know their products. In this instance Ovis was up against a competitor who had come in with a cut pile carpet at fifteen cents a square yard less than the carpet Ovis was selling. Ovis laid his sample on the desk beside his competitor's. The competitor's sample was fuzzy and tended to "pill" when the pile surface was rubbed. Ovis pointed out that his carpet was constructed of continuous filament yarn and thus would not pill and fuzz as carpet made of other constructions might. The label on the competitor's decorator board sample did not indicate "continuous filament." The wholesaler was quick to see the difference. Ovis closed his sale. Carpet is big ticket merchandise. When Ovis closed this sale by using his sample to close by comparison he earned a nice commission of $635 in less than thirty minutes.

When you use samples to close by comparison your samples will demonstrate to your customer, or prosepect, just how your product works, feels, tastes, sounds, looks, or smells. Your voice and your creative salesmanship will then close the sale by highlighting benefits and pride of ownership. This is a most satisfying way to consummate a profitable business transaction.

HOW TO LET YOUR DEMONSTRATION DO THE TALKING

There are times when the most polished speech cannot close your sale. These are the occasions when you must call upon a masterful demonstration to do the talking. The language of the sales demonstration can be forceful and convincing.

Bill Sellers operates a successful automobile agency in a competitive area near a large military installation. This man's personal production is the envy of his competitors. Obviously, he deserves all the considerable money and respect that he earns every year.

Bill conducts seminars, has regular training schedules, and holds dynamic sales meetings for his force of eager sales people. He emphasizes organized speech and a trustworthy personality, but he always points out that the way to close a sale on a shiny luxurious car is by letting a demonstration do the talking. Once the customer is behind the wheel the demonstration takes over and backs up what the salesman has been saying all along. Mr. Sellers says few sales are closed in his business until a demonstration does the talking for the salesman. It's my personal conviction and observation that this holds true in just about any business that you can name. If Bill Sellers finds it smart to use a demonstration to do the talking in closing sales to tough-minded military personnel, isn't it obvious that this is one bright way for you to close sales also?

Pete Nuccitell knows how to let a demonstration do the talking. Pete sells vacuum cleaners to housewives. The key selling point Pete uses is the ease of handling and maneuvering his sweeper around furniture, into nooks and crannies, and by small children. His sweeper has all the usual features found in household sweepers, but this ease of handling in using his brand is Pete's forte in closing a sale. Pete doesn't do all the talking about it. He takes his sweeper into the housewife's home and lets a demonstration do his talking. Pete says he may have closed a sale without a demonstration doing a big part of the talking, but he can't remember where or when. Pete not only sells vacuum cleaners himself. He also has the added responsibility (and the income that goes with it) of guiding and training other men. His demonstrations recently "talked," him into the sales manager's spot.

Recently I was a guest at a huge food show given by one of the country's biggest institutional food distributors for restaurant owners, schools, hospitals, nursing homes, and other mass food operations. I was intrigued by a salesman demonstrating and selling a donut machine from a special booth. Note this: The first thing any prospect got when he stopped at that booth was a delicious hot donut right from the donut machine. Then when this demonstration had done its talking the salesman closed sale after sale. Sure there were instruction sheets, operating manuals, and recipes all over the place, but the demonstration did the talking that closed so many sales at that show.

Whatever your product you can let a demonstration talk for you. It's a convincing way to closs sale after sale after sale.

HOW GENE FENNER CLOSED WITH SAMPLES
WHEN ALL ELSE FAILED

Gene Fenner sells pickle products by the truck load. However, he had never been able to close his sale with Rex Covey, owner of Ozark Fruit and Produce Company. This day, though, he was prepared as never before. He had four pint samples of his products chilled and ready to eat. Each pint represented one of his leading items. Before Gene went in to keep his appointment with Mr. Covey, he obtained a jar of each of the four competitive samples which Ozark Fruit and Produce stocked. Then he strode into Covey's office with his eight pints of pickles in a box under one arm and a bright scotch plaid lunch kit with a thermos bottle swinging from one hand.

"Hey, what's going on?" Rex Covey asked with some surprise.

"We're having a picnic," was Gene Fenner's ready reply.

Thereupon Gene took two neatly quartered delicious ham sandwiches from the lunch kit, then poured two steaming cups of coffee, and opened eight sample pints of pickles all on top of Rex Covey's desk. Then placing plastic forks before Mr. Covey, Gene insisted that he try both brands of pickles as they ate the sandwiches and drank their coffee. All he expected in return, said Gene, was an order if Mr. Covey found his brand of pickle products to be crisper, tastier and more flavorful than the brand Ozark Fruit and Produce had been selling.

Gene won hands down. He closed his initial sale with this creative and imaginative demonstration and earned a $1200 commission that day. Gene continues to enjoy regular and substantial business from Rex Covey's firm.

Samples will close sales for you, too, when all else fails. Dynamic, ambitious salesmen in many industries prove the truth of this every day. And once an impressive demonstration is made with the authoritative proof of samples, continued business is the rule long after the first sale is closed.

PURVES' INSTANT POINTERS ON USING DEMONSTRATIONS TO CLOSE

- It's not enough to merely show your samples.
- Imagination adds fire to samples and demonstrations.
- Don't take for granted that the customer won't like something. At least give *him* the chance to say no.
- Treat your samples with respect.
- Samples talk in a compelling voice.
- Demonstrations can close sales where all else fails.

6

How to Use Questions to Close the Sale

No doubt you have heard this old analogy that has been quoted time and time again to salesmen: "While Samson slew a thousand men with the jawbone of an ass, more sales than that are killed every day with the jawbone of a salesman."

Of course, this is a dramatic way of emphasizing that sales people can, and do, often talk themselves out of big sales. It sometimes happens to the most experienced of us. There is a way you can avoid this unnerving pitfall. Ask questions. This opens your customer up. This lets your customer shoot up little signals of what interests him most—and of what may turn him off. In any event, of this you may be sure—

SELLING IS MORE THAN TELLING

Naturally, you want to tell all about your product or your proposal. It is all-important that you do so. But selling is more than telling. Some points, some features, are bound to have stronger appeal to the customer than other points or features. The areas which have special appeal to your customer are strong closing items. Since selling is more than telling, you must use the questioning technique to uncover these closing opportunities.

Here are some questions designed to spark ideas that will sharpen you skill in asking sales questions. Adapt them to your product and your personality. Word them to fit your customer and your situation. Close sales with them.

- Have you heard about our red hot special for this month?
- Now here's something you can make a decent profit on, isn't it?
- Doesn't that fabric have a nice feel?

- Which color do you prefer?
- Is $100,000 liability protection enough, or should we double that amount?
- Did you notice the 5-year warranty?
- This "no fade" feature is an important one, isn't it?
- Isn't this a prime location?
- Aren't the houses in this neighborhood beautiful and well-kept?
- That size is comfortable, isn't it?
- How soon do you want delivery?
- These quantity discounts really add up, don't they?
- Doesn't our financing plan make it easy to own?
- Why wait? You can use the business right now, can't you?
- Did you notice the cash dividends you get along with the protection and security you need?

Questions are firecrackers that can close sales. Like all explosives, they must be used with uncommon good sense. Questions should be poised and used at the key points in your presentation. Don't let them go like a load of buckshot. Too many questions fired off the cuff early in your sales interview may limit, confuse, or even annoy your customer. Questions are potent sales tools. Like all good tools, they get the job done when wisely used. The job you want your questions to do is to close sales. With thought and practice this is what you can expect them to do for you.

Ira Farr sells advertising for the biggest television station in his town. This advertising costs money. Ira uses questions to justify the expenditure and close his sale. Here are some of the typical questions that work for Ira.

- You want to make all the money you can, don't you?
- You know that this form of advertising will give you the widest possible exposure, don't you?
- Have you seen these figures which show the tremendous influence TV exerts on the buying habits of *your* customers?
- You have noticed the high-powered program your competition is running several times a day, haven't you?
- This is high class advertising. You can appreciate what it would do for your image, can't you?
- You know this is one of today's best mediums. Don't you think it would be dollar smart to put this in your advertising budget at once?
- How soon do you want to get started?

Ira's skillful questions close enough sales with worthwhile clients to give him a high five figure income that keeps a growing family comfortable. Ira says they provide a lot of pleasurable extras that otherwise would be denied him and his family. He keeps his questions that close sales razor sharp and he hones them every day. New bright questions, he knows, keep adding to his glowing record of closed sales.

Just as hot and needling questions work for Ira they will do as much for you. Shape and form them for the greatest impact on your customers within the framework of your market and your products. *Your* questions can close *your* sales.

HOW TO LISTEN AFTER THE QUESTION IS ASKED

Asking questions to close the sale is important. Listening after the question is asked is no less important.

Here are some common barriers to good listening after the question is asked:

- Impatience to get on with your own sales pitch.
- Preconceived notions about how the sales interview is going to turn out.
- Underestimating the customer's or prospect's business sense.
- Inattention.
- Failure to recognize how much importance the customer attaches to what *he has to say*.
- Failure to recognize vital closing signals in the customer's answer to your question.

What do you do about these barriers to listening (and to the closing of the sale)? In effect, how do you listen after the question has been asked?

- Pause after a pertinent question. This indicates that you expect an answer and will respectfully listen to your customer's reply and opinion. It also gives the customer a chance to answer. Rushing on with your sales story suggests the question wasn't meant to be taken seriously. If a question is frivolous and unworthy of an intelligent answer by your customer, forget it. It can only damage your sales story.
- Keep the customer at ease. If he feels that the pressure of your

questions are testing him, he will freeze and become unresponsive. You can avoid this by forming your questions so that they involve his welfare, his designs, his needs. When your questions are given this flavor they lead your customer to an agreeable "yes." And this leads to the closed sale.

- When you listen don't overdo it. If you look too rapturous you become suspect. Polite careful listening is all that's required or expected. Listening should never be condescending.

- Remember that listening after the question is asked is a monetary matter. You profit and your customer profits when his answer speeds the closing of a mutually beneficial business transaction.

- Listen with sincerity. This way you can learn what the customer's objections or excuses are. When you hear this and offer genuine solutions to his problems you have put a handle on your closed sale.

- Avoid any hint of artificial interest or attention. If the man is smart enough to have a dollar to spend with you, he is smart enough to know if you are faking it. As an experienced salesman you won't be likely to step into this hole. But it has happened.

HOW TO USE QUESTIONS
TO FIND OUT WHAT THE CUSTOMER WANTS

What the customer *wants* is often more important to him than what he *needs*. When you employ skillful questioning to uncover his wants, the customer is ripe for the closing. Here are examples of tried and tested questions which uncover *wants*. Apply them to your sales situation and your customer will help you close your sale when you give him what he *wants*.

- Doesn't this top-of-the model car handle easily and ride comfortably?
- This is true luxury, isn't it?
- Do you like the money-saving features of this size?
- Isn't this a beautiful style?
- Aren't the security features of this proposal outstanding?
- This is a good buy, isn't it?
- You like to please your wife, don't you?
- This will drive your competition up the wall, won't it?
- How's this for prestige and status?

When questions of this persuasion are asked you can capitalize on the customer's answer whether it be positive or negative. If the response is positive you can pursue this feature to a logical closing. If the response is negative, more questions are in order until you uncover the customer want that will open the way to the closed sale.

HOW TO UNCOVER THE CUSTOMER'S NEEDS WITH QUESTIONS

The techniques employed in probing to uncover a customer's *needs* are much like the questions asked in finding out what the customer wants. However, the questions used to uncover needs are usually more basic and direct. Here's an example.

Dorrel Snyder, a realtor in one of our more affluent metropolitan areas, practically sold a $200,000 home before he so much as took his prospect out of the office. Through a series of well-planted qualifying questions Mr. Snyder quickly determined that his client could buy an expensive home. A few more questions and he uncovered the client's key need in a new home. His concern as to warmth and shelter was not nearly as demanding as his need for prestige and status. With such essential information this salesman showed his client two houses in a prestigious new subdivision. Before sundown the client's wife had indicated her preference and Dorrel Snyder had the contract and earnest money which guaranteed him a $12,000 commission. Realtor Snyder later stated that the questions he had asked to uncover his customer's needs were worth $1000 each.

Questions that you ask to uncover your customer's needs are worth real money to you. Put them to work to close more sales and enjoy your extra dollars.

HOW TO ASK THE CLOSING QUESTION

This is the one that counts. All the other questions are designed to lead right up to the closing question. Unless the closing question is asked the whole sales interview will end as a mere practice session, or an outright exercise in futility.

Here are examples of closing questions that have meant closed sales and big money to determined professional salesmen.

- This policy will make it possible for your business to stay in the family, won't it?

- Do you want the regular 30 day terms, or do you prefer the special 90 day terms?
- This proposal has everything you want, doesn't it?
- Why wait? The sooner we get started, the sooner the extra profits begin.

The most obvious question—and the most effective—is to confidently *ask for the order.* When you have completed your presentation the customer expects you to ask for the order. More often than not, he actually wants you to ask for the order. There are many productive variations of the closing question that asks for the order. Look these over for ideas:

- Will Tuesday delivery be soon enough?
- Will six dozen be sufficient or shall we make it an even gross?
- Of course, you want the bonus offer with the free goods, don't you?
- Now that we've covered everything, will you just sign on this line?
- Fortunately, we can meet all your requirements and solve your problems today, can't we? Now, if you will give me your purchase order number we can wind this up in a hurry.

Ask the closing question early and often. If you do not, you and your customer both lose. When you do everybody wins.

PURVES' INSTANT POINTERS ON HOW TO USE QUESTIONS TO CLOSE THE SALE

- Selling is more than telling.
- Questions uncover closing opportunities.
- Listening after the question is asked is more than hearing. If you just hear the words without *listening* you may miss the closing signal.
- Questions are tools that reveal the customer's wants and needs.
- Don't ask too many questions.
- Avoid questions which commit the customer to less than he wants or can handle.
- Ask clean-cut questions that leave the impression that you are the one salesman best qualified to fill your customer's needs and wants.
- Ask for the order.

7

How to Close on a Minor Point

Not all sales are closed because of sound logic and keen judgment. There are times when the obvious and best reason for buying will not sway the customer. These are among the times when a salesman must close on a minor point.

Minor points should never be thought of as something to drag out only in an emergency. They are excellent closing tools for just about all selling situations. As any dedicated pro can tell you, it is good strategy to have back-up ammunition ready in case your most reasonable appeal falls short of closing the deal. Minor points are strong reserves to fall back upon. Here is one good reason:

CLOSING ON A MINOR POINT
KNOCKS OUT THE BIG HASSLE

It is much easier for your prospect or customer to make a small decision than it is for him to make a major decision. For example, when it is apparent that the buyer is going to have trouble handling the whole ball of wax, give him a minor decision which still commits him to the closed sale. Here are minor issues often used by big-league salesmen as a basis for closing.

- Delivery dates
- Financing plans
- Premium or bonus goods
- Colors
- Terms
- Sizes
- Quantities

- Models
- Styles
- Optional features
- Advertising plans
- Leasing versus outright ownership

These, and the additional minor points that you can adapt to your product and your customer, will knock out the big hassle of a major decision.

Jerry Whalls remembers when he kept trying to sell a truck load order of sofas to Harlan Furniture Company. Mr. Harlan seemed interested enough, but couldn't quite bring himself to say "yes" no matter how much Jerry urged and prodded. Finally Jerry said, "Could you handle a dozen assortment right now?"

Mr. Harlan said "yes" to this minor point and the sale was closed promptly.

Minor points call for minor decisions, but they can close big sales for you.

HOW TO MAKE THE MINOR POINT A BIG DEAL

When your big gun doesn't get the job done you must make the minor point a big deal.

It is hard to imagine a product or sales proposal that doesn't have at least a few attractive minor points. The response your customer makes to your sales presentation will quickly uncover the minor point he likes. When he ignores the issue that looks the biggest and best to you, your alternative is to make the minor point a big deal. You do this, of course, by emphasizing the minor deal while the main theme rests in the background.

Marge Norman is one of a new and growing breed. She is a salesman, or more properly, a salesperson. She sells new cars. Recently, she had a man and his wife who insisted that the car be a four door in a certain expensive model. Marge's trained ears soon learned, however, that a light shade of pink was the color preferred by the wife. Now there wasn't a four door model on the lot, but there was a two door model up front which just happened to be a lovely light pink color. Every time the question of a four door model came up Marge diplomatically called attention to the beautiful pink two door—all serviced and ready to go. Marge gave the wife the keys and invited the couple to try the pink car. When they returned the husband said, "Okay, we'll take it. She likes the color and I think we can make it in a two door anyway."

Marge succeeded in making the minor point of a pink color more important than the big issue of four doors and closed the sale. With variations, salespeople make the minor point a big deal and thereby close sales on the spot every day.

HOW TO KEEP THE MINOR POINT BOILING

Every time a sale is closed there is always one key issue that has swayed the balance. Often it is a minor point. The salesman who takes advantage of this money-making fact closes sales that otherwise would be postponed or lost forever. Note how Harold Messerly closed an impressive real estate deal on a minor point.

Hal had been showing homes to his prospects, Mr. and Mrs. Barry Reinker, for two days. The Reinkers were being transferred from Cleveland and were well qualified to buy. Mr. Reinker had placed a $100,000 ceiling on the amount he would spend for a new home. However, the only house his wife liked was listed at rock bottom price of $150,000. But it did have a wonderful garden spot in the back yard. This was Hal's key, for he knew Mr. Reinker had checked each place for a garden. Mr. Reinker had explained that he didn't golf because he liked to spend his spare time in his garden. Hal had recognized this well-publicized closing signal. He made the most of it. He purposely managed to drive near the house with the garden three times the second day. Each time he stopped and urged Mr. Reinker to have another look and to recheck the garden plot. Hal had a strong ally in Mrs. Reinker. On the third day Mr. Reinker decided that since this was the house Mrs. Reinker wanted they would buy it. But Hal and Mrs. Reinker knew why he had decided to buy the house. That minor point—the garden spot—had closed a $150,000 deal. Mr. Reinker had his garden. Hal had his $9000 commission.

Hal kept the minor point boiling by going back to it time and again. He closed his sale by this technique. It will happen to you, too, when you keep the minor point bubbling and boiling.

HOW TO USE THE MINOR POINT
TO OVERCOME OBJECTIONS

Hal Messerly's case validates another truth: You can use a minor point to overcome objections. Mr. Reinker objected to paying more than $100,000 for his new home until Hal made that garden spot his key

to whipping the objection. Of course, once the objection was laid to rest
the sale was closed.

Keep Hal's performance in mind. You can utilize his experience next
time you run into a stiff objection. The minor point you discover can
overcome objections and close your sale.

Ken Slade, a fence salesman in the open spaces of the Midwest,
focuses his customer's attention on the minor point of the method of
payment. He lays the total dollars and cents proposition before his
customer after the type of fence and the erection plans have been completed. Then, before the customer can make the major decision of taking the whole package, Ken asks his customer what payment plan he
prefers, cash, 90 days with no interest, or a bank finance plan. When
this decision is made it does two things: It heads off, or overcomes any
price objection; and it closes the sale.

Ken says that it is not uncommon for him to earn from $500 to $1000
per sale—and that most of them are closed on this relatively minor
point. That is worth more than a passing thought from any salesman
interested in substantial money.

HOW TO DRAMATIZE THE MINOR POINT
INTO A CLOSED SALE

When you lay hold of a minor point, dramatize it until it becomes a
closed sale. Here's how:

- Lead your customer back to it at every turn.
- Support your main point by tying the minor point to it. For example, an elderly couple bought a new piano—not because the new
  piano was a bargain (as it was) but because the salesman
  dramatized how much their granddaughter would enjoy playing
  for them on a *new* piano.
- Emphasize the benefits and pleasures the minor point affords.
  (Remember Mr. Reinker's garden spot?)
- Make the minor point a plus value. It's a benefit *in addition* to the
  main sales point.

When you dramatize a minor point you can expect dramatic
results—and nothing is more dramatic than a healthy closed sale.

PURVES' INSTANT POINTERS ON
HOW TO CLOSE ON A MINOR POINT

- Not all sales are closed on the basis of sound logic and keen judgment.
- It's easier for your customer to make small decisions on minor points.
- Small decisions on minor points lead to closed sales.
- Minor points can be made into big deals—which close big sales.
- Once you latch onto the minor point keep it boiling until the sale is closed.
- Minor points overcome objections.
- Dramatize your minor point into a closed sale.
- Support your main point with your minor point.
- Closing on a minor point makes it easier for your customer to say "yes."

8

How to Close by Finding Areas of Agreement

One of the hallmarks of a successful closer is the knack of finding areas of agreement that make it easy for customers and prospects to sign the order. Outstanding salesmen know this.

YOU DON'T HAVE TO AGREE ON EVERYTHING BEFORE YOU CLOSE

Fortunately you and your customer or prospect don't have to agree 100% on every detail of your product or proposal in order to consummate a satisfactory sale. It takes only one point of agreement to close. Watch Fred Buckner use a point of agreement to close a $1,000,000 key man insurance sale.

Fred was interviewing Mr. Reece Levin, president of Levin Garment Manufacturers. He was making no progress because Mr. Levin said he already had more insurance than he needed. Then Fred asked, "Who is the most important man in your business, Mr. Levin, besides you?"

Mr. Levin answered promptly that it was Marvin Taylor, his executive vice-president.

Further questioning by Fred revealed that the only insurance on Marvin Taylor was a nominal $20,000 which the company group policy provided. Mrs. Taylor was the beneficiary of that policy.

"How much would it cost you to replace Marvin Taylor?" Fred asked instantly.

Mr. Levin replied that Taylor was a $1,000,000 man and would be extremely difficult to replace.

"In that case," Fred pursued this area of agreement, "you need at least $1,000,000 worth of insurance on Mr. Taylor just to guarantee that your business will remain intact in case something should happen to him today."

"You're right," was Mr. Levin's concerned reply. "How soon can we get him covered?"

Mr. Taylor passed his physical the next day and the policy was put into effect. Utilizing this one area of agreement also put a $20,000 commission into Fred Buckner's pocket.

When you come up with an area of agreement in your sales presentation, jump on it with both feet. As Fred Buckner's case illustrates, you don't have to agree on everything in the book before you can close a sale.

DO THIS TO UNCOVER AREAS OF AGREEMENT

The selling process cannot be separated from the buying process. Until the buyer (your customer or prospect) agrees with the salesman (you) in at least one area there will be no sale. The sale must be made in the mind of the buyer. The salesman is ready to close the sale. He cannot close his sale until an area of agreement penetrates his customer's thinking.

Since customers (buyers) do not always understand exactly why they make buying decisions, or what motivates them, you cannot find an area of agreement by blurting out, "Well, what do you like?" This probably would only make the customer defensive or hostile. But the alert and experienced salesman will quickly detect areas of agreement from the subconscious signals every customer shoots out.

A customer is signalling areas of agreement to you when:

1. He asks if repair parts are readily available.
2. He expresses concern for safety.
3. He talks about making money.
4. He talks about saving money.
5. He wants to know who else has one like it.
6. How the item is packaged.
7. What fabric is used.
8. What colors are available.
9. Is there a larger size.
10. How long has your company been in business.

There are unlimited ways in which a customer may signal you an opportunity to uncover an area of agreement. As a starter, let's analyze the foregoing one by one.

In item number one, the customer is really saying, "If you can convince me that repair parts are readily available I'll agree to buy your equipment." The competent equipment salesman will recognize this signal and quickly seal off this area of agreement with back-up proof that, indeed, repair parts are readily available for his equipment. He will discuss and display service records to show how well he and his company perform in that category. He will suggest that the customer call one or two of his satisfied customers (at the salesman's expense) and verify his statements. Then he will ask for the order and close his sale.

Number two may have had some recent bad experience and safety assurance is the area of agreement that will close his sale. The salesman will handle this signal much as the equipment salesman in item one handled his. And, of course, as any well-versed salesman would do, he will close his sale on the basis of the area of agreement.

When number three talks about making money, the area of agreement he is laying open to the salesman is *profit*. He is saying, in effect, "Show me that I can profit from your deal and we will close this sale."

Making money is one of the strongest of appeals. When the salesman is working in this area of agreement, the green lights are flashing all around. In this case all the prepared salesman has to do is show how and why his deal will make his customer money. Then he can promptly close his sale.

Number four is a more conservative type than number three, but he still has the same thing on his mind—money! The business-like salesman will offer convincing assurance that his proposal or product will indeed save his customer money. His clinching reasons for buying will be much like those offered by the salesman in number three. Like all salesmen who are prepared to look for and utilize areas of agreement, he will close on this area.

Number five probably is prestige conscious. His ego needs feeding. The salesman who is prepared to satisfy this area of agreement with this type customer is ready for the close. All he has to do is name the business or community leaders who have bought the product. Like all areas of agreement, when this one is uncovered and recognized it leads to the closed sale in short order.

Number six is revealing an area of agreement. He is saying that if the packaging fits his needs he will buy. Here the salesman will show how the product is packaged, how easily it stacks, what an appealing display it makes, and how the unique and attractive package will generate store traffic and increase sales. When the area of agreement which this question uncovers is answered positively, the closed sale is at hand.

Number seven is revealing that the fabric represents the area of agreement that will close this sale. When the knowledgeable salesman uncovers this area of agreement, he will show his samples, identify and extol the merits of his fabric, and close his sale.

When number eight asks about colors he is saying, "Help me agree on a color and you can write the order." This area of agreement is a simple one. When you find yourself in this area about all that's left for you to do is help the man select his color and close your sale.

Number nine is signalling that if you can provide the larger size you have reached an area of agreement that will close the sale. Give him the larger size and go home with your closed sale.

Number ten is saying, "Show me that your company is stable and sound and we can close a lot of sales from here on in."

To close in this area of agreement requires that you clearly recite your company's history, explain its assets and resources, and ask for the order. In this instance, romance your company's history, but avoid a lengthy torrent of words. Stick to the vital facts the customer needs to nail down the area of agreement. That will close your sale.

Often areas of agreement must be ferreted out with questions. The customer's answer to your questions, his facial expression, his tone of voice, his request to handle your product, or to look closer at your idea or proposal, can uncover areas of agreement for you. The main point is to act when an area of agreement is uncovered and lock up your closed sale then and there.

HOW TO MAKE THE AREA OF AGREEMENT
BIGGER THAN THE OBJECTION

Even the best of salesmen encounter objections day after day. However, the pros rise to this challenge and close sale after sale right in the teeth of objections. One of the tested and effective methods used by these men to combat objections is to find an area of agreement and make it bigger than the objection.

Delbert Hutchins has sold life insurance for more than twenty years. He is one of the experts at uncovering areas of agreement and making them bigger and much more important to his customers and prospects. Here's how he closed a satisfying sale by employing this technique.

Delbert had prepared a proposal for a $50,000 whole life policy on the life of his prospect, Clyde Orr. Mr. Orr was prosperous enough to buy adequate insurance, but he had stated that he didn't believe in insurance, that the premiums were too high, and that he was plenty healthy anyway. But Delbert's adroit questioning had already uncovered two vital areas of agreement. Number one: Cylde Orr needed to protect his family from economic disaster, and number two: Clyde Orr wanted each of his three children to attend the college of his choice.

Delbert had also determined that Mr. Orr had made no adequate provision to protect his family, nor to educate his children as he seemed determined to do. In fact, Clyde Orr seemed to be a little embarrassed at his lack of foresight as Delbert kept skillfully guiding the conversation around the objections and back to the area of agreement. At this point Delbert put the application in front of Mr. Orr and said, "Mr. Orr we both agree on the importance of protecting your family and providing for your children's education. In fact, you yourself said that those were the two most important things you had to do. Sign right here and you will have taken care of both these problems tonight."

Clyde Orr forgot his objections and signed. Delbert Hutchins had made the areas of agreement much bigger than the objections. He had every right to his closed sale because he knew how to make the area of agreement bigger than the objection.

HOW TO IDENTIFY CLOSING SIGNALS
THAT THE AREAS OF AGREEMENT SHOOT OUT

The very act of finding an area of agreement is a booming closing signal. An area of agreement conditions your customer to say "Yes." It's hard to say "No" to someone when you are in agreement with him. You can safely identify and claim every area of agreement as a closing signal.

You have a closing signal any time a customer shows interest in a point you've made in your sales presentation. He doesn't have to stop you and say, "Now wait, I'm interested." You know your customer is interested when he asks questions, nods in agreement, asks you to go over a key point, takes your sample for a closer look, or carefully checks a proposal you've made. These and numerous other closing signals will be shooting your way as you uncover areas of agreement. Close your sale as soon as you identify one of them. There will be no better time.

HOW TO MAKE TIME AND TIMING
AN AREA OF AGREEMENT

Every fire-balling salesman is concerned with time. The aggressive and experienced salesman knows that how he manages his time will largely determine the results of his day's work. Busy customers and live prospects must also entertain a high regard for their time. "Time is money," you've heard over and over again. And you know it's true. Time is a prime ingredient in the skillful marketing of any product. You can make time and timing an area of agreement in your strategy to close more sales. Here are a few ideas that will help you hit the target in your own field of operations.

Matt Henry always calls on the headquarters of World-Mart Associates, a buying group, just before the Chicago Housewares show. Often just before a market a salesman will by stymied by the vague promise, "I'll see you at market." It is well and good to see your customers at market. But such promises don't close sales before market time. Closed sales are needed all the time. Matt Henry operates on this thesis. That is why he calls on World-Mart Associates just before market.

This pattern started several years ago when Gaylen Connors, Matt's contact with World-Mart, said, "I'll see you at market."

Matt wanted to close his sale then and there, so he made this point into an area of agreement with this reasoning: "The best time to buy my merchandise is now, Mr. Connors. We are one of your major suppliers," Matt reminded, "and I have all our market specials for you. Let's do this part of your market shopping right here and now. You'll get the same program we will have at market. When we write your order for my merchandise today you will have that much more free time to work the other departments of your business at market. Doesn't that make sense to a man as busy as you are?"

Mr. Connors had to agree. Matt closed his sale when he made time and timing an area of agreement. These before market orders for this buying group are never for less than a straight carload. Matt says it's a mighty good feeling to go to market with $700 or $800 in commissions already tucked away under your belt.

"Inventory coming up" is another putoff that lends itself to using time and timing as an area of agreement to close your sale. Harry Rose, who was my tutor and supervisor when I was a bright-eyed and bushy-tailed twenty-four year old, gave me the key to handling this problem. "Give them price protection and a dating if necessary," he said. "Then write the order for after inventory delivery." He could have said make time and timing an area of agreement and close your sale. But I got the idea and have used it profitably ever since.

There are countless other put-offs that can be licked when you make time and timing an area of agreement to close your sale. For instance:

- When a customer wails, "I don't have that kind of money just now!" you can work with your credit department to extend him terms if he is a sound operator. Or you can use case histories to show how other customers have met this problem and bought the goods to keep their business on the high profit side of the ledgers. When this agreement is reached that means that now is the time to close your sale.

- One ambitious salesman always showed up at eight o'clock sharp at a busy wholesaler's place. He kept getting the brush-off until he realized that everybody in the place did nothing else until their fifteen trucks were loaded and on the road. When he made an appointment to come back at ten o'clock he gained an audience that eventually led to many closed sales. It's easy to see that his eventual success was a matter of making time and timing an area of agreement so that he could close his sale.

- John Moffitt has a standby statement for the customer who says, "I don't need any right now." John says, "What kind of a reason is that for not buying! You know you will need it. Let's write the order and be sure you have the merchandise at the time you do need it."

    John makes time and timing an important area of agreement and closes many sales weaker men would wait to close.

Not every man's idea will close every sale for you. You are an individual. As a capable, experienced individual you can enlarge upon the expertise of your peers and close many extra sales by making time and timing an area of agreement.

HOW AREAS OF AGREEMENT GIVE YOU THE UPPER HAND

Each time you find an area of agreement you strengthen your position as an authority. As an authority you are in charge. And the man in charge always has the upper hand in the vibrant give and take of an exciting sales encounter.

Joe Morriset was making his third call on Big Land Lumber and Pallet Company. He felt that he had almost sold his $50,000 automatic crane each time. This time he meant to finish the job. On this third interview he was reminded again that $50,000 was a lot of money. But when Joe produced written proof that one of Big Land's competitors in an adjoining state had increased product delivery 225% with his crane he had an area of agreement. Richard Namsfield, president of Big Land, couldn't deny that this was indeed something he should consider. Then, when Joe showed that a saving of $8,000 annually would accrue as a result of this kind of increased efficiency, he had another overwhelming area of agreement.

Joe knew that he had the upper hand with *two* big areas of agreement. His keen business judgment told him that now was the time to close his sale. All he had to do was ask for the order. His next commission check supported his good judgment to the tune of $2,500 extra.

Areas of agreement will give you the upper hand as they did Joe Morriset. Areas of agreement melt objections, eliminate doubt, convince the customer, and smooth the way to the closed sale. Take full advantage of it when an area of agreement gives you the upper hand. This is another way to close big sales fast.

PURVES' INSTANT POINTERS ON HOW TO CLOSE BY FINDING AREAS OF AGREEMENT

- **You don't have to agree on everything before you close.**
- **It takes only one point of agreement to close a sale.**
- **The selling process cannot be separated from the buying process.**
- **An area of agreement must be uncovered to complete the selling process.**
- **You overcome an objection when you make the area of agreement bigger than the objection.**
- **An area of agreement is a booming closing signal.**
- **You can make time and timing an area of agreement to close your sale.**
- **An area of agreement gives you the upper hand.**

9

How to Close by Being a Problem Solver

More and more today's salesman is the man who is expected to give professional advice along with his goods and services. The professional salesman of today is a professional problem solver. It is true that the modern up-to-date salesman must know more about many aspects of his customer's business than the customer himself does. Assuredly, he must know more about his product and its applications then any of his prospects or customers do. This is not an unreasonable demand. Indeed, the pace setters in present-day selling look upon this as an opportunity to get more than their share of an ever-growing market. They know that the better informed a salesman is the more effective he is as a problem solver. And the better he is at solving his customer's problems, the more sales he will close.

HOW TO RECOGNIZE A CRY FOR HELP

True, a smart customer will ask his salesman for help. Businessmen, merchants, and progressive people in all walks of life regard salesmen as experts in their field. The day when a salesman needed only a glib tongue (if, indeed, there was ever such a time) has long been gone. Today, he must be a consultant — a problem solver — if he expects to survive long enough to close many sales.

While your customer may come right out and ask you to help him with a troublesome problem, you must still be prepared to recognize a cry for help that may not be in the form of a direct request. Frequently, you will have to point out your customer's problem as well as to provide the solution for him. Many times the problem goes undetected until some helpful salesman points it out. The usual reason for this is that if a customer — or prospect — is plugging along in a comfortable little rut he may not be aware that there is a better way of doing something, that there is an improved product, or a more efficient procedure. These unrecognized hazards can prove deadly to your customer friends. When you encounter such situations you can close impressive sales by recognizing and responding to your customer's unspoken plea for help.

Lynn Gilder recognized a cry for help, earned a $500 commission on a closed sale, and made a valuable customer of what had been a borderline account. Lynn's customer, Garden's Decor, sold drapes, accessories, floor coverings, and related home furnishings. The weakest link in Garden's product line was what should have been his biggest ticket item — carpeting. Lynn was a manufacturer's representative specializing in carpet. He sensed Garden's concern and on the next call, after careful preparation, presented Mr. Garden with the money-making solution to his silent cry for help.

Garden's Decor maintained attractive and orderly displays of everything that they had to sell except for one department. That department was carpeting. Despite the splendid potential afforded by carpet sales, the carpet department was a jumble of disorganized samples and decorator boards. No rolls were stocked. Apparently Garden's waited for lightning to strike, then ordered anything sold from samples which they kept around. This presented another problem. Their carpet samples were so neglected that sales were lost because the samples were still being used even though a number of the styles and fabrics had been dropped by the mills.

Lynn answered Garden's cry for help by asking for thirty minutes to explain how Garden's carpet sales could be improved and the department pyramided into the top money-maker for the store. Lynn used his thirty minutes to point out that Garden's relied on too many overlapping qualities, failed to keep track of current styles and fabrics because of the disarray and multiplicity of samples, used more sources than they could keep track of, and failed to stock any roll goods for customers who demanded instant delivery. Mr. Garden had to agree that not only he, but his retail customers as well, were often confused by the jungle of samples and the difficulty of plowing through such a confusing mass of colors and styles.

In the end Lynn agreed to help Garden's eliminate unprofitable and slow-moving items, and to outline an orderly sample and display program for Garden's. In turn, Garden's gave Lynn an order for ten rolls of carpet for floor stock, plus an order for current samples.

Lynn closed his sale by being a problem solver when he recognized a cry for help. You can close sales the same way when you look for, listen for, and recognize a cry for help. Below are some of the more obvious distress signals that will tell you your customer is sending out a cry for help to you.

Your customer is screaming for your help if any of the following applies:

- His displays are sloppy and poorly lighted.
- His back-up stock is in disarray.
- His product knowledge is skimpy.
- He is out of touch with current trends and styles.
- He is operating below his potential.
- His equipment is obsolescent.
- His record keeping is inadequate. (Yes, this too. Your customer must be a good all-around businessman if you are to close worthwhile sales regularly with him.)
- He has trouble taking his discounts.
- His accounts receivable are in arrears.
- His inventory is out of balance.
- His mark-up is too low or too high.
- His inventory turnover is below normal.
- His personnel lacks training.
- His planning is slipshod.

You can close additional sales and earn extra money by recognizing these and the many other cries for help. These pleas for help enable you to act as a dependable consultant to and for the people you work with day in and day out. And consultants close sales.

HOW TO BE A DEPENDABLE CONSULTANT

The mechanics of being a dependable consultant may vary in style and form from salesman to salesman and from customer to customer. The substance will always be the same. Here are basic guidelines that the professional salesman-consultant will always respect and adhere to.

- Give advice and help only where you are confident and qualified. Never try to fake it.
- Be watchful and alert to uncover areas where you and your product will solve a problem or fill a need.
- Talk to your customer as an equal.
- Speak and act with all the authority at your command. Your customer's respect is essential to your role as consultant.

- Keep up-to-date. Read. Attend seminars. Study. Contribute to sales meetings.
- Be *the* expert on your product and in your field.
- Fulfill every promise.
- Keep every date.
- Know what your customer's competition is doing.
- Put your customer's interest up front. He has to prosper to help you prosper.
- Don't play games. The purpose of being a consultant is to close more sales. Fill your role as a consultant with that thought on the front burner at *all times.*

Andrew Bentley sells and conducts motivational courses. His courses are structured to make salesmen and managers more effective. In the process, these courses also help strengthen weak spots in personality and character.

Andrew had a friend, Guy Swanson, who owned and operated a large plastic pipe manufacturing concern. That is, the manufacturing facilities were large. But the personnel in the plant and in the field were in a constant state of flux. At the country club in which both men were active members, Guy Swanson complained bitterly to Andrew about this problem. It was more than an annoyance; it was an added burden and expense, said Swanson. This was the opportunity Andrew Bentley had been waiting for. He had approached Guy Swanson several months earlier, but Mr. Swanson said nobody in his business needed "motivating." Now Andrew was in a position to exercise his role as a dependable consultant and close his sale.

"Guy," he said, "I can tell you bluntly and exactly what's wrong and how you can eliminate that problem. Further, I can tell you that it is not going to get any better until you do something about it. You could have been out of the woods three months ago if you had listened to me earlier."

"I'm all ears at this point, Andy," was Swanson's reply.

Over another cup of coffee Andrew Bentley made his points direct and clear. First, he said, there was no screening test for new employees. Guy did all the hiring by the seat of his pants. Next, Andrew drove home, there was no appreciable training program. Furthermore, no matter how many employees Swanson had brought in, he was still going like a whirling dervish and trying to cover every detail himself. Guy hammered at the fact that he was setting an impossible pace for himself, and limiting his firm's real growth to only what he could personally keep his fingers in. All the while he was a disagreeable, unhappy man on the job. No wonder good people left him after a few weeks of frustration and jangled nerves!

"Okay, what's the answer," asked a thoroughly interested Guy Swanson.

Andrew answered, "This twenty minute consultation hasn't cost you anything. But I can have you and your crew working as a team if you agree to take my two-week course I've already explained to you. I'll put it on personally, but only if you agree to attend every session yourself. You are the key to the problem. The cost will be $300 per man. Including you, that will be fourteen people. I can guarantee it will be the best $4200 you have ever spent."

"That's pretty stiff," said Guy Swanson, "but if it solves my problem, I'm your man from now on."

Of course Andrew Bentley performed exactly as he promised. Guy Swanson had to agree that he earned every bit of his fee of $4200. The twenty minute consultation had been a bonus. Guy never forgot it. To this day he still turns to Andrew Bentley as a dependable consultant. And Andrew is still closing sales by being a dependable consultant at every opportunity.

Whether you are selling electrical components, fresh eggs, environmental control products, or what have you, you can close sales by being a dependable consultant just as salesman Andrew Bentley did when he closed his sale as a problem solver.

HOW TO MAKE THE MOST OF YOUR EXPERIENCE

Customers and prospective customers alike respect the experience that a journeyman salesman has gained. The fact that a man has survived and prospered in a tough and competitive profession is evidence enough that he has learned some valuable lessons. The way to make the most of your experience is to put it to work to close sales that will benefit you and your customers. Your customers will be confident and at ease as they rely on the seasoned judgment of an experienced businessman.

Here are a variety of methods to use as you make the most of your experience to close sales that spell big money.

- Use case histories as clinchers to close sales. Few things are as convincing as proof supported by factual stories and examples. These true life stories are especially exciting when they detail what a sincere salesman has done to help his customers as he closed sales profitable to all parties.

- Share the promotional ideas that your more successful customers
  have used to generate extra business. Every time a slow mover uses
  such ideas that you bring him, the more business he will do. This,
  along with his improved financial condition, will open the door for
  you to close more sales with him.
- Use your authority as an experienced businessman to control your
  sales interviews. As the authority in charge you have every right to
  close your sale.
- Take advantage of the extra product knowledge your experience
  has given you. The expert is always a strong closer.
- Use your experience to brush aside put-offs and objections. The
  man who has been through the fire can quickly identify excuses
  and stalls. He is also equipped to close his sale in the face of such
  invalid tactics. Call upon your experience in such instances and
  close your sale just as all pros do.

HOW TO CLOSE BY BEING THE EXPERT

As we have already noted, the expert is always a strong closer. There
are sound reasons for this. The expert is a respected man. His peers
listen to him and have confidence in what he says. This is an undeniable
asset when it comes to closing sales.

Roy Hutchinson is an expert in real estate appraisals. Recently he
had a prospect who wanted to buy a parcel of land for a huge retail
supermarket. The plot of ground was priced right at $200,000, but Mr.
Hutchinson moved his client up and closed a sale for $500,000 and
made a fast 10% commission. He did this by showing his client that,
while his site selection was fairly priced, it was not the best buy for him
at any price. Hutchinson used population shift figures and projections
for the next ten years prepared by the utilities companies to show his
client that the $200,000 plot of ground was in a declining area. He
recommended the $500,000 piece of ground on this basis. It was expert
advice and closed the bigger sale. Mr. Hutchinson's expertise not only
earned him a heftier commission on his closed sale, but kept his client
from making a costly blunder.

The expert is a problem solver. The expert solves problems in order
to close sales.

YOU GET EXTRA DIVIDENDS
WHEN YOU CLOSE AS A PROBLEM SOLVER

Extra dividends accrue to you when you close your sales as a problem solver. To list a few:

- Your customers will provide you with referrals.
- You will always have an attentive audience.
- The problem solver always has the edge on competition.
- You can maintain charge of your sales interview.
- You can stay on top of the customer until your sale is closed.

Austin Dillard is a knowledgeable merchandiser. He knows that you get extra dividends when you close as a problem solver. Here's a classic case from the experience of this money-making salesman.

Austin is an independent manufacturer's representative with three lines. One of his volume lines is a popularly priced lamp and lighting line. A customer of his, Heartland Lamp and Electric, seldom ordered over two dozen lamps at a time. This was miniscule in comparison to Heartland's total volume. Austin decided to do something about this problem. He cited the volume he enjoyed on his lamp line and led Heartland into agreeing that they should be enjoying more sales on this lamp line. Then Austin made the proposition that he was sure would solve this problem of low volume. He explained that his manufacturer would park a trailer truck load of lamps on Heartland's lot for a "Truck Load Sale," and he, Austin Dillard, would be on hand the Saturday the sale was held to help sell the lamps. All that Heartland had to do was advertise the lamp sale heavily the week prior to the sale. Heartland agreed. The sale was closed. The extra dividend Austin earned on this and repeat orders amounted to $5001.00 before the year was over.

Claude Fleetwood sells flavors and extracts. A big segment of his business comes from the ice cream and dairy products industry. Before Claude went on the road he was an ice cream manufacturer. Recently he made the most of his experience, closed a sale as a problem solver, and landed a new customer. This particular manufacturer was having trouble with his chocolate ice cream. It wasn't freezing to the desired consistency and was somewhat gummy. Claude quickly discovered that the chocolate product being used was loaded with sugar, and much more suited for the soda fountain than for use in a freezer. One trial convinced the manufacturer that Claude knew what he was talking about. Claude has every reason to believe that this customer should develop into a worthwhile account.

When you make the most of your considerable experience to close as a problem solver you can expect to land new accounts just as Claude Fleetwood does.

PURVES' INSTANT POINTERS ON CLOSING SALES BY BEING A PROBLEM SOLVER

- The professional salesman of today is a professional problem solver.
- Frequently, you will have to point out your customer's problem as well as provide the solution for him.
- You can close sales when you look for, listen for, and recognize a cry for help.
- Today's salesman must be a dependable consultant.
- You can put your experience to work to close sales.
- The expert is a problem solver, and the problem solver closes sales.

10

How to Use Emotional Appeal to Close

If every sale could be closed on the bare bedrock of pure logic and sound reason, about all you would need to close your sale would be a handy little pocket computer or calculator. But that is not the way it works.

Emotion is often stronger than reason. There has never been a buyer so hard-nosed that he has never bought anything on the basis of emotional appeal. Nor has there ever been a professional salesman so cold-blooded and methodical that he never sold anything except through sheer logic and overwhelming reason. We can all be glad for that. Professional selling is a humanistic undertaking involving personalities and the surge of human emotions. Without that the profession would lose much of its zest and flavor. Able men would seek more exciting fields, and intelligent buyers would be bored to tears.

YOU CAN'T CLOSE EVERY SALE WITH PURE LOGIC

You can't close every sale with pure logic no matter what your product or your program may be. Indeed, if sales were closed exclusively on this basis few, if any, warm-blooded, ambitious salesmen would be needed. A little fact sheet with neat rows of figures and carefully tabulated features could be mailed the prospect or customer and presto! A closed sale.

This is not to say that logic and reason do not matter in closing a sale. Far from it. Logic and reason are prime motivators. In fact, when you close a sale it must be logical—logical from the point of view of your customer. Emotional appeal often opens the door of logic in the customer's mind.

Life insurance salesmen, for example, understand the power of emotional appeal. They appeal to the prospect's strong emotional ties to his family to induce him to buy the right amount and the right kind of insurance. They build up the prospect's concern for the welfare of his loved ones and when the emotional appeal has done its job they close the sale. Then everybody has what they want. The family has the protection they need, the father is emotionally gratified that he has provided for his family's welfare, and the salesman has his closed sale.

It has been said that there are three main types of buyers, namely, the individual buyer, the family buyer, and the organizational buyer. None of them are totally emotionless. Each and every type of buyer will respond to the proper emotional appeal. Emotional appeals are complex. The human being is a complex creature. It would be an impossible task to list every emotional appeal and to catalog every precise situation where it would close your sale. But as a successful businessman and a student of human nature (as every salesman must be), you will recognize which emotional appeal to utilize to close your particular sale. To speed up the process here are some of the basic emotional appeals that star salesmen use to close tough sales and earn fat commissions.

- Appearance
- Contentment
- Speed
- Power
- Recreation
- Pride
- Sentiment
- Sex
- Personal friendship
- Security
- Health
- Success image
- Comfort
- Companionship
- Love
- Fear
- Emulation
- Gain
- Curiosity
- Duty
- Beauty
- Style
- Convenience
- Safety
- Hate
- Romance
- Self-image
- Relaxation
- Pleasure
- Esthetic motives
- Ambition
- Ego
- Self-esteem
- Respect
- Prestige
- Dignity
- Influence
- Leadership
- Acquisitiveness
- Status

As a rule, buyers are rational. This is especially true if the buyer is a professional, i.e., a businessman, or a professional buyer on somebody's payroll. Nevertheless, emotional appeals are there and working automatically for every salesman who will tie them in with logic and reason. The partial list given here, plus a multiplicity of other emotional appeals, are keys to the closed sale.

Chad Ekkers had finally made it. He had come up the hard way in the trucking and drilling business. Now he was middle-aged and affluent. He wanted the world to know it. He and his wife had just moved into a new $500,000 home. In their search for furnishings they had visited the Kindworth Art Galleries several times and looked at the original works of a number of artists. Mr. Ekkers had balked at looking at anything over $5000 even though he had more money than he had ever dreamed of in years past. By the time they came back in for the fourth time Charles Kindworth, senior partner in Kindworth Art Galleries, had gleaned a great deal of information about Mr. Ekkers. On this day he put that information to work and closed a sale totalling $50,000 for two paintings. He closed with emotional appeal aimed directly at Mr. Ekkers. When he did this his firm earned a 35% consignment commission on the art work sold. That is $17,500 for closing one sale with emotional appeal. Here's how Mr. Kindworth did it.

When Chad Ekkers came in and again walked to the $3000 to $5000 paintings, Charles Kindworth went over and said, "Mr. Ekkers, I know that you are a successful businessman. You have demonstrated that you have excellent taste merely by coming to an art gallery to select decor for your new home. May I show you something that I think will be most fitting for a man in your position? These works have esthetic charm which will give you and your guests much pleasure. This artist's work is hanging in some of the most prestigious homes in New England. I'm sure that you will agree that he is a master with a warm touch. He is much in demand. We have only two of his paintings now. Either would add elegance and color to your magnificent new home as well as being an excellent investment."

Chad Ekkers wrote a check for both pieces of art work. Here is why:

Salesman Kindworth had hit pay dirt with emotional appeal. He had at one and the same time—

- Used the success image appeal, the self-esteem appeal, the emulation appeal, the appeal of pride, the esthetic appeal and the appeal of ego, status and fear.

Let's take a clearer look at each.

Chad Ekkers was conscious of the fact that he was not a professor, or other professional man, but he wanted the image of success associated with such men. Mr. Kindworth bolstered Chad Ekker's self image when he sold him the two paintings with the success image appeal. The merchandise was worth every penny it cost as far as Mr. Ekkers was concerned.

The self-esteem appeal is akin to the success image appeal. Kindworth knew that self-esteem is important to all men, but particularly to those who have worked hard to achieve success. As you see, it was a most potent closing appeal in this case. It is always a strong closing tool.

Mr. Ekkers wanted to identify with leaders. Kindworth used the emulation appeal. Naturally it strengthened his case and hastened the closed sale. You will note that Mr. Kindworth was careful to mention that this artist's work was hanging in some of the most prestigious homes in the area. The paintings would allow Mr. Ekkers, the implication was, to join and emulate these leaders. The appeal worked. The sale was closed.

Charles Kindworth used the appeal of pride wisely. Here was a famous artist sought after by society's best. Anybody would be proud to own his works. The salesman stirred the emotional appeal of pride in Chad Ekker's chest. It worked. The sale was closed without more lost time.

Of course, the esthetic appeal was made. Mr. Kindworth assured Chad Ekkers that the paintings would add elegance and color to his home. Mr. Ekkers was a sensitive man. These paintings would prove it. So Mr. Kindworth had the closed sale.

Charles Kindworth played on Ekker's ego. These paintings would cause him to be recognized as a man of refinement as well as a man who owned a fleet of trucks and a well drilling rig. Ego is a strong appeal. The closed sale proved it.

The appeal of status is heady stuff. Mr. Ekkers wanted status. Mr. Kindworth recognized this. So he used this appeal as an added incentive. It did its part in closing the sale.

The appeal of fear was also employed by Charles Kindworth. See how subtly he used it.The artist was popular. His works in demand. Mr. Kindworth had only two pieces of his work. Somebody else might buy them. This appeal closed the sale on two paintings instead of only one.

Of course, logic was presented, too. The paintings were a good investment. The tie-in played its part in closing the sale. Emotional appeal backed with a modicum of logic is hard to beat when it comes to closing a sale.

When you have a sale to close consider the many emotional appeals that sway buyers. They represent a powerful closing technique. Whether you use one or a range of appeals as did Mr. Kindworth, you can close your sale with emotional appeal, and you can often do it with emotional appeal when other techniques fail to work.

HOW TO MAKE EMOTION A DECISIVE FACTOR

When logic and sweet reason fail, that is a clear signal to close your sale with an emotional appeal. You can make emotion the deciding factor when you detect an emotional signal from your customer. You have your signal when his face lights up as you mention status, prestige, comfort, leadership, and so on. You have your signal when he shows interest in safety, health, or any of the dozens of emotional appeals that your product or proposition can offer.

Here is a case in point:

Emory Tucker is a top-notch office supply salesman operating in the Midwest. Two years ago the president and owner of a large restaurant and institutional supply company retired and turned the business over to his son. Now Emory had been trying to sell Zeke Russell, the father, a new desk for years. But old Zeke had made a lot of money behind that cluttered simple desk he used, and he felt resentment at the suggestion that he really should have a new and larger desk. However, Emory had met young Russell and knew the youngster needed an ego booster more than anything else. So he called on Johnny Russell just about as soon as the young man was handed the reins. He showed him glossy pictures and drawings of his biggest, most efficient all-metal desk. He explained that this desk denoted leadership, efficiency, authority, and was a hallmark of the successful business executive. There was no quibbling over price. Johnny's only question was, "How soon can I get it?"

Though Johnny knew that his dad had made a mint behind the old relic he had willed to Johnny, the son's emotional needs made a new desk logical from his point of view. And in truth, it was logical — it filled a basic need for Johnny Russell. Emotional needs and emotional appeals are strong stuff. Emory Tucker, a seasoned salesman, closed his sale by making the emotional appeal the decisive factor. Johnny Russell is still sitting happily behind that big shiny desk today.

HOW TO USE EMOTIONAL APPEAL
TO SOFTEN THE TOUGH CUSTOMER

The toughest customer you will ever meet craves recognition from his fellow man. He also wants to feel that he is of some importance. He may shrug it off outwardly, but he wants to be complimented and appreciated just as do less crusty men.

The foremost thing to keep in mind when you are dealing with the tough personality is this: Don't do all the talking. When the tough customer is talking and blustering *he feels important*. When you let him feel important he will like you and you will have the inside track to the closed sale.

This is not to imply that you should remain mute during the whole encounter. You are obliged to present your case forcefully as always. But to close a sale with the tough customer you use indirect methods more often than you do under normal circumstances. Let him talk and compliment him when you can honestly do so. Do not resort to flattery. Let him feel appreciated and competent as you lead him to the closed sale.

Ed Fullmer, a big time hard goods salesman, always begins the interview with a tough customer by complimenting him. That is not a difficult thing to do, Ed says. He maintains that he can always warmly and honestly compliment the toughest customer. This persistent and powerful salesman explains that he compliments this type on such items as a clean inventory, his keen judgment in selecting personnel, his no-nonsense attitude, his finely organized office, his grasp of current business problems, his sound judgment, and even the sparkling shine of his shoes or the clean cut of his suit.

You can soften the tough customer by making him feel important, appreciated, and competent. This is how Ed Fullmer closes sales with tough customers. This is one good way that you can use to close your sale when you are face to face with a tough customer. And a sale to a tough cookie pays just as much commission as a sale closed to the sweetest guy in your territory.

HOW TO USE EMOTIONAL APPEAL
TO GET ACTION FAST

Recent years have seen a great growth in the appreciation of how human emotional patterns affect marketing and marketing men. Smart salesmen study and utilize the selling force and strength of emotional appeal. One of the strongest of these appeals is the emotion of fear. A trait that is common to us all is to want anything that is hard to get. This "hard to get" theme has been exploited by salesmen in every field. The emotional appeal of fear of loss gets action fast.

People normally do not buy things without a reason. This is why educated, experienced, trained salesmen are ready to use emotional appeal to start the ball rolling. The emotional appeal *fear* will get a slow mover off dead center and on the way to fast action. Fear of missing the boat — not getting the benefits the salesman extols — is sufficient reason to enable the business-like salesman to close his sale without delay.

I know a New York Life salesman who had the life of an accountant friend of mine insured. The accountant kept the books of a large auto and tire service center. One day he unexpectedly died of a heart attack even though he was less than fifty years old and apparently in good health. Of course, New York Life promptly paid his widow the sizable amount of insurance the accountant had on his life. Two weeks later The New York Life salesman had sold new life insurance policies to two young men who were also employed at the auto center. The New York Life salesman had given them plenty of opportunity to buy before. Yet it took the emotional tug of *fear* to move them to action.

One industrial salesman sold a factory two new machines by using the appeal of fear. The old equipment used by this firm had been breaking down with some regularity. Parts were hard to come by on these models and repairs were slow. This alert salesman first proved that parts were readily available on his new models and that his company maintained an efficient and eager service department. When he utilized this fear factor and convinced the customer he was the man to handle the problem the *fear appeal* closed the sale on two new machines. Industrial machinery is not cheap. The salesman's commission on this sale was $25,000—earned by getting action fast on the emotional appeal of fear.

These are two examples of how to use emotional appeal to get action fast. You, too, can get fast action with this emotional appeal. When the timing is right use it and collect your richly earned commission along with the gratitude of your customer.

PURVES' INSTANT POINTERS ON HOW TO USE EMOTIONAL APPEAL TO CLOSE

- **You can't close every sale with pure logic and sound reason.**
- **Emotional appeal makes the closed sale logical from the point of view of your customer.**

- Professional selling involves the surging force of human emotions.
- Emotional appeals are keys to the closed sale.
- Emotional appeals are often the decisive force in closing a sale.
- Emotional appeals can soften the tough customer and lead him to the closed sale.
- The emotional appeal *fear* can get action fast.
- Use emotional appeal when the timing is right and collect your commissions on the closed sale.

11

How to Close with Enthusiasm

As everyone who has served his apprenticeship in selling and marketing knows, enthusiasm is a subject that has been offered more than once as a panacea for all the sales problems extant. It has been suggested that enthusiasm alone is all that is ever needed to close any sale. I hold that it is not quite all this.

Enthusiasm is important, yes. It is a vital factor in closing sales. But there must be some meat on the bones. The salesman who fares forth into the reality of the market place with nothing more than a balloon of enthusiasm is not going to close many sales. Sales enthusiasm must be based upon substance. The sales manager who relies only on an evangelistic enthusiasm does his salesmen and his firm a disservice. Enthusiasm, to be healthy, useful, and sustaining in the art of closing sales, must have roots. It must be rooted in product knowledge and product applications that inspire confidence. Enthusiasm built upon these business bones will be exciting, productive, and enduring. It will close sales for you.

The salesman who does not support his enthusiasm with study, product knowledge, and basic selling techniques, will be disappointed at his lack of closed sales. The salesman who uses personal enthusiasm as added power to enhance his product knowledge and his basic sales techniques is going to set the woods on fire.

What is this prized ingredient enthusiasm? One apt dictionary definition that I like is "strong excitement of feeling; ardor." The same dictionary, the newest edition of which I just purchased from the bookstore at Drury College, defines an enthusiast thus: "One who tends to give himself completely to whatever engages his interest."

It has been estimated that only ten percent of the national sales force enthusiastically does its best. Can you imagine how many more sales would be closed every day if all salesmen and sales executives had "strong excitement of feeling: ardor," and "gave themselves completely," to closing the sale? Why the GNP would go out of sight if this happened!

Now let's look at what enthusiasm is not. Enthusiasm—if it is to close sales—is not artificial. It is a genuine feeling that the salesman has for his product and his service. It is the sincere communication of intense conviction that leads to the closed sale. It is not so shallow as to be a series of bold gestures and loud vocal fireworks. Many powerful closers display their enthusiasm with a fervor as smooth and quiet as a bass fisherman's.

We have examined enthusiasm a bit. Everybody realizes that closing sales without enthusiasm is about like getting the proverbial camel through the eye of the needle. So what do you do about it?

HOW TO GENERATE ENTHUSIASM

Not everyone is born with a bubbling, excitable personality. Not every salesman or sales manager exudes enthusiasm as naturally as he breathes. But personality can be developed; enthusiasm can be generated.

If you feel that you are just naturally not the enthusiastic type, take heart! You can generate a real head of enthusiasm by practice and study. Of course, there is a lot of acting in selling. The man who chooses selling as a career is certain to have some ham hidden somewhere in his make-up. Professional actors practice, rehearse, study. Professional salesmen must do likewise to become enthusiastic performers and producers.

Study your product and the services it performs *even after you know it all.* Practice your sales presentation before your wife, your mirror, or the bare walls. Rehearse what you plan to do and what you plan to accomplish. As your confidence grows in these private sessions, so will your enthusiasm. Then you are ready to go out and enthusiastically convince others that your proposition is vital to them. Your personal infusion of enthusiasm into the act of selling will make the closing easier and more satisfying for all parties.

Hubert Matson was nearing forty when he decided to quit his job as a route salesman. He felt that his opportunity to make real money lay in big ticket sales. His particular route job had little potential for growth. So Hubert had made up his mind to go to work for a large investment house. He started as an account executive selling a portfolio of mutual funds. His first month was less than spectacular. He went to his sales supervisor for help.

Richard Mansfield had been watching Hubert closely. He got right to the heart of the matter. First, he pointed out to Hubert that his previous job called for a minimum of enthusiasm. This was because Hubert called on the same trade regularly, and had been obliged to do little creative selling. Most of his time had been devoted to checking his customer's inventory and want list. Then he brought in the needed items. Selling mutual funds was entirely different. Mr. Mansfield explained that Hubert would have to be a much more enthusiastic salesman to sell thousands and millions of dollars worth of merchandise, as opposed to what he could carry in his arms from a truck.

Then he outlined a program for Hubert's weekend. He was to practice being enthusiastic. Hubert looked skeptical, but agreed to follow the program to the letter. He was to report the progress of his concentrated practice and rehearsing at lunch with Mr. Mansfield the next Monday.

Richard Mansfield was already seated when Hubert arrived at Cheong's Tea Room, a busy Chinese Restaurant in the heart of the city. Mr. Mansfield was pleased to note the new spring in Hubert's step. His face had lost its deadpan look. He could hardly wait to tell Richard Mansfield what he had learned. His enthusiasm boiled all through the meal. He spoke glowingly of what he had to offer his clients. Mansfield enjoyed the lunch immensely.

Mr. Cheong owned three restaurants. He spent the noon hour mixing with customers at this one. He had visited Hubert's table and stood quietly listening. Then when Hubert and Mr. Mansfield went to the cash register Mr. Cheong followed. He tapped Hubert's shoulder. "I would like to know more of the exciting investments of which you speak so enthusiastically," he said. "Could you come back at three o'clock when it is not so busy in here?"

Hubert floated out the door. At 3:30 p.m. that day he made his first $100,000 sale.

Hubert had generated enthusiasm not only in himself, but in Mr. Cheong. His enthusiasm was not fake. It merely needed the fire that Hubert's earnest practice had given it.

Practice and rehearsing will generate enthusiasm where none existed. It will add sparkle and glow and power to the enthusiasm you now possess. Put it to work as Hubert did. It can close big sales for you.

HOW TO USE ENTHUSIASM TO INSPIRE CONFIDENCE

If a salesman hopes to close a sale he must be able to inspire confidence in the buyer. Nobody inspires confidence in another unless he first has his full share of self-confidence. Ask yourself: Have you ever bought anything worth mentioning from a salesman who was shot through with self-doubt, bored, or indulging in self-pity?

Enthusiasm breeds self-confidence. As we have pointed out, practice generates enthusiasm. The whole secret of self-confidence is to act enthusiastic. When you act enthusiastic and excited, you will become enthusiastic and excited. This is sound selling psychology. This is a firm basis on which to build self-confidence.

Enthusiasm is a practical, business-like application of self-confidence that inspires confidence in the buyer. When you use enthusiasm in this sense it will close sales for you.

Most men and women who are competent enough to land a sales job are smart enough to analyze their personality problems. A young college graduate was so dismayed by his feeling of inadequacy over his failure to close sales as he knew he should that he had decided to go to a psychiatrist. But then he made up his mind that he was not a helpless blob. His self analysis turned him around. He saw that his failure to close sales was not the reason for his debilitating sense of inadequacy. In fact, he clearly understood that, in reality, his unenthusiastic outlook, his feeling of inadequacy, was the reason for his poor ratio of closed sales.

It has been four years since this young graduate told me of his experience. He is now a vice-president in charge of marketing and sales training for a successful direct selling organization. He says his success came quickly after he vowed to practice and use enthusiasm to build confidence in himself and others. The motto on his desk reads: "Enthusiasm is Action."

Enthusiasm in action inspires confidence. Enthusiasm in action closes sales.

HOW ENTHUSIASM KEEPS
YOUR CLOSING POWER FIRE-BALLING

The best of salesmen have bad days. The difference is that they never let their enthusiasm wane. They have learned that a slump is not the end of the world. They know that the surest way to snap out of a slump is to maintain their enthusiasm. The way to maintain your enthusiasm is to act enthusiastic at all times. When you *act* enthusiastic you can't help but *be* enthusiastic. And your enthusiasm will keep your closing power fire-balling.

The legendary Frank Bettger said, "I firmly believe enthusiasm is by far the biggest single factor in successful selling."

That's a pretty heady statement. But who wants to argue with success? Mr. Bettger's long record of closed sales is evidence of his success and of his authority. He could very well have said, "I firmly believe that enthusiasm is by far the biggest single factor in keeping your closing power fire-balling." It all adds up to the same thing.

Gary Umphries, a case goods salesman for over twenty years, likes to tell how he learned about enthusiasm and how it keeps his closing power going full blast.

Gary's first job was as a furniture salesman working for a small manufacturer in the south. After nine months on the job he was summarily fired. At first he was angry and upset. He started to stomp out and say good riddance, but he knew there had to be a reason for his dismissal. He was intelligent enough to think it might be to his advantage to at least know why he had been sacked. So he asked his sales manager why he was being fired. The answer he received set him back on his heels.

"Because you are lazy and disinterested in your job," was the sales manager's blunt reply.

Gary vehemently denied this. He honestly felt that Joe Whittleton, his sales manager, was wrong. His protests did little except to bring forth a question from Joe Whittleton. Mr. Whittleton asked, "Then why is it that you never showed any enthusiasm? You moved about with indifference. Your ratio of closed sales to calls indicated you were lazy and disinterested. For nine months we let you bring up the rear. I would say you had a fair trial, wouldn't you?"

Gary said it was late at night before he could bring himself to admit that Joe Whittleton had made an honest appraisal. Though Gary was not a lazy man, nor an indifferent one, his selling pattern had left that impression. Gary reasoned that if Whittleton had formed a wrong opinion of him because of his unenthusiastic work patterns, then countless customers must have done likewise. He says this realization was a bitter pill, but that it proved to be good medicine.

Within a week Gary had a new job with a growing furniture manufacturer. He says that he didn't wait until he had the job to act enthusiastic. Rather, he explains that he practiced being enthusiastic before the job interview. He is sure that his enthusiasm during the interview paid off for him. Gary was selected from among eleven applicants.

Gary has continued to make enthusiasm a part of his selling personality. It has kept his closing power fire-balling. For example, last year he led the sales force with closed sales of over two million dollars. His earnings topped $100,000 for the first time. Mr. Whittleton would like to have Gary and his enthusiasm back on his team.

HOW ENTHUSIASM HELPS CLOSE *PEOPLE*

When you close a sale you must first close (convince) somebody. It's been said that you don't sell things, you sell people. Buying decisions involve human emotions. When a customer or prospect is exposed to a salesman who radiates enthusiasm, he responds in kind. A sale is much easier to close when there is excitement in the air. As any experienced professional can attest, enthusiasm on the salesman's part generates excitement. The salesman who puts the magic power of enthusiasm to work is going to close sales. The people that he calls on won't have it any other way.

Here is a battery of questions. Give them the test of candid self-criticism. Your answers will tell you how well you are using enthusiasm to influence people into the closed sale. Your strictly personal answers may also help you to improve your ability to close people.

- Are you enthusiastic in your desire to be of service?
- Are you enthusiastic about solving your customer's problems?
- Do you wax enthusiastic over what you and your product can do for your customer?
- Are you enthusiastically fair-minded?
- Do you use enthusiasm to help your customer make the best possible buying decision?
- Are you obviously enthusiastic about improving your customer's welfare and business?
- Do you maintain enthusiasm when your customer is grumpy or unreasonable?
- Do you enthusiastically expect to close every sale?
- Are you enthusiastic about your own person?
- Do you maintain control of your emotions and act enthusiastic under pressure?
- Do you enthusiastically support your firm's policies?
- Do you enthusiastically review product knowledge?
- Do you enthusiastically work to close (convince) people?

Enthusiasm is not a crutch to help you deal with people. It is the ball of fire that gets people excited. It is the competitive edge in closing sales. If your answer is "yes" to these searching questions, your enthusiasm is already working hard and will close sales for you.

HOW TO FOCUS YOUR ENTHUSIASM ON THE CLOSING

Enthusiasm, like any powerful force, must have purpose and direction. No matter how sincere and genuine your sales enthusiasm is, it will avail you nothing if it is not directed at the closing. Enthusiasm is wonderful in any personality, but in the sales personality its purpose is to close the sale. Focus it on the closing from beginning to end. Here's how, step by step.

First, go in with enthusiasm. Let your face, voice, and manner show that you are pleased to be face to face with your customer. This way you create an air of expectation. It's exhilarating to be in an arena where you feel that something exciting is about to break into the routine of a work-a-day world. Your customer, or prospect, will be caught up in your spirit of enthusiasm. He will want to see what it is that has you wound up and ready to go.

Second, not with a shout and a dance, but with precision-like enthusiasm bolstered by product knowledge, business sense, and a sincere desire to improve the welfare of your customer or prospect, you begin your demonstration. The demonstration may be nothing more than a chart of statistics projecting an expected return or profit. But this calls, too, for the maintenance of a high degree of personal enthusiasm. Your enthusiasm must enable your customer to visualize the returns your project has for him. Let your enthusiasm rub off on him so that his mind's eye will see the benefits that your proposition will bring him.

If your demonstration (which is the process of showing your customer what has you wound up and enthusiastic) is a physical product, then really turn the showmanship on. As you explain and handle the product, share the center stage with your friend. Let him handle, operate, taste, see, feel, and smell it. If you have done your homework you can help and encourage his enthusiasm every step of the way as he becomes more and more involved in your demonstration. When his interest and enthusiasm peaks, that is the time to move into step number three.

Number three is the key step—the closing. Here you quickly and enthusiastically recap your main sales features, re-emphasize the benefits your product or proposition will afford your customer, and ask for the order.

Of course, as an experienced and observant salesman, if you see buying signals before the whole presentation is finished, you will close in the middle of the performance. This has happened more than once when an enthusiastic, competent salesman has generated the excitement and interest that speeds a closed sale. Every time it happens to you, you will know that you have a handle on a mighty potent sales tool—an enthusiastic sales personality.

We have some beautiful streams in the Ozarks. I've lost a few lures in them myself. Recently I was replenishing my tackle box in a local sportings goods store when a salesman came in with a dozen new lures in a plastic box. Under his arm he carried an empty aquarium. I stood back to watch. This guy must have been one of the world's most enthusiastic fishermen. Assuredly he was a most enthusiastic salesman.

First, he came in like the fish were biting. He wouldn't open his new lures. Instead, he laid them on the counter and said to Bob Archer, the proprietor, "Look at these beauties while I fill my tank."

Then he came back with his glass tank full of water, took the lures out one by one, snapped a short line on them and pulled them back and forth in the water. He talked excitely of their color, their life-like action, and how the fish would go for them. He had Bob pull them back and forth and feel the action as he listened to the gurgling sound they made to help attract the big bass.

Next he asked for the order. I don't know how much money he made on that sale, but I'm sure that was not the last sale he will close with Bob. In fact, I got in on the act. I was Bob's first customer on the new lures. Enthusiasm is contagious. If I don't catch any fish with these lures those fish just have to be crazy!

PURVES' INSTANT POINTERS ON CLOSING WITH ENTHUSIASM

- Enthusiasm won't replace product knowledge—but it will make your product knowledge glow and sparkle with interest.
- Enthusiasm won't change company policy overnight—but it will make your firm's policy seem reasonable and proper.
- Enthusiasm won't take the place of study—but it will make it an inspirational exercise.
- Enthusiasm does not do all things—but it will:
    Create excitement
    Generate interest
    Add fire to your sales presentation
    Eliminate boredom
    Reinforce sincerity

Put conviction in your speech
Demonstrate personal interest
Give life to the abstract
Support the concrete and physical
Remove doubt
Get the slow mover off dead center
Close sales.

12

How to Close on a Choice

Here is a point that you should always have in mind as you work to close any sale: you are a part — a vital part — of your customer's business function. No matter what you may be selling you are not merely a spectator. You are more than a casual observer. Further, as a part of your customer's business you are obliged to help him make the right choices.

Decision making can be unadulterated torture for many people though they be highly intelligent and experienced individuals. Buyers are no exception. The decisions they must make on a daily basis can be excruciating. Not only is their job at stake, but the welfare of the whole group that they work with is affected by their buying decisions. It is a heavy responsibility. As a knowledgeable and conscientious salesman you share this responsibility. Giving your buyer-customer a choice can take a lot of the agony out of decision making. When you help him make the right choice you not only shoulder your part of the responsibility, but you have also closed your sale.

One thing that is important to remember when you are closing on a choice is this: Don't overwhelm the customer with a multitude of possible choices. This will only delay the closing. Instead, eliminate the choices that do not represent an opportunity to close your sale promptly. Select the choices that meet your customer's requirements, offer the needed benefits, and knock out further stalling.

Methods of restricting the choices can be utilized whether your product is tangible or intangible. If your physical product comes in fifteen assortments, give your customer a choice between the two that are most appropriate for him. If you are selling securities select two or three, and don't talk about the great variety available from all sources. Naturally, in selecting choices you will be careful to decide on only those that you feel will effect a quick close and, at the same time, fulfill your customer's wants or needs.

HOW USING THE CHOICE METHOD MAKES IT EASY
FOR THE CUSTOMER TO SAY "YES"

As an experienced salesman you have heard most, if not all, of the thousand and one put-offs and excuses that buyers use to avoid making decisions. "I want to think about it first." "We have inventory coming up." "We don't have much room." "I want to check your deal over first" — translation, "I want to see if I can use your big-hearted deal to beat your competitor over the head and bleed a little more out of him." And so on and so on.

Now, since it is obvious that making a buying decision can be difficult for many good people, it is to your advantage to make the process easy. When you give your customer a choice you make it easier for him to decide. When he decides you have your closed sale.

Bill Letz sells tools and equipment to contractors and builders. Recently he called on Powers' Concrete Company, a firm that does much work for the city where Bill lives. Powers' also does many jobs for prime contractors, industry, and other firms. On this particular trip Bill was trying to close a sale on a concrete grinder. A concrete grinder is a machine that mows down rough spots on concrete floors, patios, sidewalks, or other concrete surfaces. Bill had covered all the desirable features on his machine, such as, the 8 H.P. engine, precision tapered roller bearings, 70 pound ballast with safety chain, and adjustable wheels for easy mobility. Powers' was apparently well pleased with these features as well as the water shut-off with three foot hose and the tapered front to allow close viewing of the work. But he still hadn't given Bill the order.

At this point Bill gave him a choice. "Which do you want, the mowing head with ten segments of industrial diamonds at $1295.00, or the mowing head with twenty segments at $1620.00, either of which we can deliver today?"

Powers said, "Twenty segments, of course. We like to work fast."

With that Bill wrote the order, Powers signed it, and the machine was on the job site by late afternoon.

Bill explains, "Hank Powers is big and tough as iron, as you can see. Yet he detests decision making. His account nets me twelve to fifteen thousand dollars a year, but he never buys until I give him a choice. The choice makes it easy for him to make up his mind and say yes. It sure works better for us when I come up with a choice. It takes the pain out of it for Hank and it gives me my closed sale."

One sales consultant once vowed that executive suites, buyers' offices, stores, shops, and businesses of every ilk, were filled with people who squirm and suffer when they are faced with decision making. "That is when they come to me," he said. "My job is to make it easier for them."

As an expert in your field, as a prosperous and conscientious salesman, you can make the decision making process easier for your customers. You do this by giving them a choice. When you do they will reward you with closed sales and repeat business.

HOW TO USE A CHOICE TO GET THE BUYER TO CLOSE THE SALE FOR YOU

A lot has been said about getting the customer involved in the sales presentation. A sales presentation has but one purpose. Its purpose is not to entertain your customer or prospect. Its purpose is not to fill in gaps of time in the salesman's day, or to afford him an opportunity to show how bright and capable he may be. The sole purpose of the sales presentation is to close the sale. When you involve your customer in your presentation you can get him to close the sale for you by giving him a choice. In the final analysis, you cannot close a sale without customer involvement. He *wants* to be involved if you have given him anything at all to arouse his interest. Involve him by giving him a choice. As you lead him with your experienced judgment to the right decision, he will make an intelligent choice, and thereby lay the closed sale in your hand.

Lawrence D. Braddy of Cardon Adhesive and Tapes works the manufacturing trade. His key customer is Great Sauk Wood Products. It took him three years to get his first order from Great Sauk. He says that when he did, it was really Ben Ocker who closed the sale. Ben Ocker, Great Sauk's buyer, was satisfied with the adhesive he had used for years. He was courteous enough to Larry, but never bought his first order until he closed the sale himself. Here's how it went.

Larry had repeatedly detailed the advantages of his adhesive to no avail. Then one day he laid a brochure before Ben Ocker saying, "This product is available in sizes ranging from tubes to barrels. The larger the size, the better the price. Look at the choices you have." Then he left again without the order.

The next morning Mr. Ocker called bright and early. "Say, Larry," he began, "the adhesive I've been using is good, but available only in sizes no larger than five gallon pails. I've tested your product. It's Okay, and the fifty gallon drum price represents a real savings. Do you think you could deliver us 1000 gallons on the tenth of each month? If you can do that, I have your first order on my desk as soon as you want to pick it up."

Larry lost no time in picking up that order. He says it's an automatic sale now — the only difference is the order keeps growing.

"Ben Ocker closed the sale, but give the devil his due," says Larry. "I made the choice of a bigger unit available to him."

Give your customer a choice. When you do you may just get him to close the sale for you. Larry says one such closing can easily add hundreds of dollars a month to your income.

Don Coe, who has sold toys to chains and mass merchandisers for years, has some definite opinions on using a choice to get the buyer to close the sale for you. "The tougher the buyer is," he states, "the more likely he is to demand that he is the one to close the sale. I give my buyer a choice of items, packaging, delivery, advertising and display pieces, or anything that will make it easy for him to decide what will best do the job. Then I ask "which" not "if." When the choice is made, my buyer has closed the sale for me. This is an excellent technique to close any time with anybody, but the meaner the buyer the better it works. It takes the pressure off him, and it takes the pressure off me. We are both happy when the sale is closed."

HOW A CHOICE DEMANDS A DECISION

When you ask your customer to make a choice you are not asking him whether he wants to buy or if he had rather forget the whole proposal. You are asking him to do something. You are asking him to buy something then and there. The more careful you are in the choices you elect to make available to him, the more he will buy, and the bigger your closed sale will be.

A choice demands a decision because you are not asking the customer to do something or nothing. You are asking him to do something or something. You are saying, in effect, the choice is to be made by you. Which do you want? It is not a question that leaves a gate open and swinging for your customer or prospect to go through and away. It is a question that demands a positive answer. This question demands a commitment. When the customer makes his choice the sale is closed. That is the time to write the order.

Marvin Hollingsworth is a veteran salesman in consumer products. He sells shelf items. This merchandise needs display and advertising if it is to hold its own with the crushing competition it has. Marvin calls on a variety of customers, but, as you would know, his major accounts are the big shooters in the business — super drug stores, discounters, supermarkets, and chain accounts. Marvin is aware that many of these buyers are besieged by salesmen each day. He knows decision making, with its inherent risks, can become painful to them. He has found that giving them a choice that demands an answer works with these busy buyers. He varies his choice according to his promotions and the customer. Here is one he likes especially.

When Marvin maps a program for one of his accounts, the amount of dollars involved is substantial. However, on these quantity purchases (which seldom net Marvin less that $1000 per sale) his firm has a co-op advertising plan. The plan is not available on lesser orders. Marvin always presents both deals — first, the heftier one with the professionally executed co-op advertising tie-in, then the lesser deal that is merchandise-only with regular terms. As he puts the proposals before the buyer he stresses the advantages and pulling power of the co-op advertising plan. He, as a matter of course, details the dollars the buyer's firm will save when the co-op plan is chosen. He offers testimonials and success stories relating to his high-volume plan. Then he asks, "Don't you agree that the co-op plan is the best buy for a store with the traffic and business you have?"

Marvin's customers select the co-op plan nine times out of ten. You can see that as Marvin poses the choices that demand an answer he works to make it easy for the buyer to select the one that represents the fattest closed sale. Anything less would be an injustice to Marvin's firm, his customer, and his own potent sales ability.

Don't sell yourself short. Use choices that demand an answer. You and your customers will enjoy the prosperity of sales closed on this basis.

HOW TO LIMIT YOUR CHOICES FOR A QUICK CLOSING

In this matter of selecting choices for a reasonably quick closing, you must make some choices of your own ahead of time. You will have to limit the choices you lay before the man, else you might be there all day trying to help your customer unravel a ball of confusion. Too many choices lead to exasperation. What your customer needs is the best possible choice for him. When you weed out all but two or three (two is better), you cut out the deadwood. An essential part of closing a sale is respecting your customer's time. Throwing out the excess choices does this.

The veteran salesman who has been doing his job well is always sure of a warm welcome from his customers. They are gratefully aware of the in-depth knowledge he has of their business. They know that they can rely on the choices he selects for them. When an experienced salesman calls on a new prospect or a new account, he lays the groundwork first. He learns all he can about the new customer before he makes the first call. He gathers information relative to his new friend's needs, wants, aims, and potential. This important information is available from non-competitive suppliers, banks, trade associations, chambers of commerce, observation, and the salesman's own keen judgment. Armed with this information, the experienced salesman does not shoot in the dark with the faint hope of hitting something. He selects the products, promotions, price ranges, and ideas and programs that offer the best possibilities for a quick closing. Then he goes in with the best choices to close his sale and establish an enduring and mutually profitable relationship. This procedure will work for you no matter what your class of customers may be — mom and pops, individuals, giant operators, syndicates, or you name it. The basics of limiting choices for a quick closing are the same. The procedure and style may vary with circumstances, but the essentials are static and unchanging.

An encyclopedia salesman who lived in the same apartment building where I lived said he always gave his clients a choice of what to buy, not whether to buy. Hs wasn't a door-knocker who merely hoped he might find a live prospect. He gathered data on the family first. When he made his approach he knew the number of school age children in the household, and he knew something of the family's ability to pay. When he made his compelling presentation he invariably closed by laying his contract book before him for all to see, and said, "We offer this tremendous educational set with twenty-four sections and a new up-date edition each year. Or it is available without the up-date edition at a slightly lower cost. Which do you prefer for your family?"

My neighbor came home with the order including the up-date edition more often than not. When the up-date program was not chosen he made a note to go back and sell the up-date program the following year. His idea of limiting his choices to two instead of getting involved in financing, delivery, bindings, and other possible choices, must have rewarded him handsomely. I do know that he paid his rent on time and drove a new car every year.

Paul Marley sells equipment to poultry processors. His units cost money and his average commission on a closed sale runs well into four figures. He goes over the advantages of his deal and his equipment. He discusses price, delivery, and every pertinent point. But he limits his closing choices by saying, "Can your people set up this equipment, or do you want our engineers to put it in line for you?"

Paul is now part-owner of his firm, but he still makes it his business to impress each salesman with his method of limiting choices for a quick closing. He knows it works.

When you close on a choice, limit your choices as Paul does for a quick close. It will work for you as it has so often for him.

HOW TO KNOW WHEN TO CLOSE ON A CHOICE

As a salesman grows more expert he begins to automatically pick the closing technique best suited to his customer and the business environment he is thrust into. This takes time and practice. The signals are there. The experienced eyes and ears of the master salesman pick them up and transmit the best method of closing to him.

There are signs that tell the salesman when to close on a choice. Here are some of the more obvious.

When you have made your presentation, re-capped the main points and advantages, and find your customer still wavering, that is a clear signal to close on a choice. When your customer has not said "No," yet continues to straddle the fence, that is a signal that he needs and wants positive help in order to reach an intelligent decision. In this case narrow his options by giving him a choice between the two best proposals you can make. In fact, you can often narrow the choice to one. You do this by detailing the extra benefits of the one choice you have selected for him. The other choices are still there to back you up as you concentrate on the one choice most likely to move your customer off dead center. You can fall back on them if you must, but your customer is going to be swayed by the one that will benefit him most. Offer him this choice and close your sale.

Another time to close on a choice is when price has become the primary consideration. Offer the customer the best qualities you can for the lowest price. If he must choose on a price-only basis, lay your cheaper deals before him and let him have a pick. It's not ideal, but it will close your sale.

When your competitor has muddied the water, and your customer insists on seeing what you have in the same category, the time is ripe for closing on a choice. Put the items he is demanding to see before him. Right by them lay what you know he should buy. But if he is resolute in his opinion, let him choose, and close the sale your competitor would have had otherwise. You will still have the better deal tomorrow. Then you can close your next sale on the upgraded choice because, in all probability, he will have seen that the choice you suggested was the wiser after all.

CHECK LIST

Here are questions to ask yourself about closing on a choice. If your answer is "yes" to each of these, you have a handle on a fine closing technique.

- Do I make sure the prospect or customer agrees with each choice I select for him? Example: Do I condition him to say "Yes?"
- Do I know what choices motivate my customers?
- Do I listen for clues to determine the best possible choice to close by?
- Do I test the tough customer's willingness to buy by giving him a choice?
- Do I ask the stalled customer to make a choice?
- Am I alert to signals that say "close on a choice"?

PURVES' INSTANT POINTERS
ON HOW TO CLOSE ON A CHOICE

- **As a vital part of your customer's business function you are obliged to help him make the right choices.**
- **Choices make the buying decision easier for your customer or prospect.**
- **When you get your customer involved with a choice he will close the sale for you.**
- **Choices demand decisions.**
- **Limit your choices for a quick closing.**
- **Knowing when to close on a choice is a key to a successful closing.**

13

How to Use the "Fast-Action, Low-Vocabulary" Technique to Close

Every profession has specialized tools which it uses to accomplish its purpose in the most efficient manner and in the shortest time possible. The surgeon has his scalpel, the artist has his brush, the carpenter his saw, and so on. Words are the special tools of the salesman. His closed sales are dependent on how well he masters and uses these tools.

Words, like other high-speed electrifying tools, require care in handling. The same power saw that trims and shapes raw lumber into beautiful cabinets and furniture will maim and cripple if used carelessly. Words must be chosen and delivered with thought. Careless words lose their zip and power. They are misinterpreted. They can fray interest, and they kill closed sales.

We have all observed this phenomenon. Two salesmen will work the same city or territory. They will be selling the same product under identical conditions. One will be cynical, defeated, dead but breathing. The other vibrant, winning, alive, successful. Why the extreme difference when each man has the same opportunity? Let's look at their vocabulary. The words they use paint two different pictures.

The loser grumbles words of failure, fatigue and discouragement. He rationalizes his lack of closed sales by saying business is bad. His plant or firm won't ship, the billing department can't bill, and his sales manager is an insensitive slob. His customers are cheapskates and his territory rotten. His deals are no good and his prices out of line.

Look at the words he depends on!

Failure	Can't
Fatigue	Insensitive
Discouragement	Slob
Bad	Cheapskates
Indifferent	Rotten
Incompetent	No good
Won't	Out of line

You reveal your sales personality through your vocabulary. Words of gloom and defeat, as above, close no sales. Strike them from your lexicon of business language. Give them no room in your mind and heart. They are malignant.

Now let's look at the winner and the words that he uses to express life and success. He speaks of opportunity and bright prospects. He says business is growing and works to make it so. His plant or firm is on the ball. His shipping department gets the orders out. The billing department is prompt and accurate. His sales manager is intelligent and helpful. His customers are cooperative and his territory great. His deals are the best, his prices fair and competitive.

Look at the words this salesman relies on.

Opportunity	Intelligent
Bright prospects	Helpful
Growing	Cooperative
Works	Great
On the ball	Best
Gets the orders out	Fair
Prompt	Competitive
Accurate	

Obviously, the winner works with and thinks with fast-action, low-vocabulary words. His words are strong, encouraging, and alive. They are not fat lazy words. They are working words that shape attitudes and close sales.

For years I have observed two salesmen working adjoining states. One has reached mandatory retirement. I know his company's officials. They are planning a retirement party for this salesman. His record of closed sales is exemplary. He has long been afflicted with diabetes, failing vision, and broken bones. Frequently his wife has had to drive for him. But his vocabulary has been healthy. His company appreciates him. He will receive awards and honor at his farewell party. He will retire a happy and fulfilled man.

His friend in the adjoining state was fired recently. His language put him against the wall. He is over six feet tall, has the physique of a football player, and an impressive appearance. But his words leave a trail of gloom and despondency. His customers grew weary of it. This was reflected in declining closed sales. Finally his company despaired. Do you wonder?

HOW TO USE WORDS THAT CREATE STRONG DESIRE

Low vocabulary does not denote a weak vocabulary bordering on illiteracy. It means using plain easy-to-understand grammar. It means taking advantage of strong working words that create desire and close sales. It indicates developing speech with a business flavor and quality.

Your speech must have three qualities in order to create strong desire and to be an effective closing tool:

- It must consist of familiar, understandable words.
- It must be limited to your customer's interest.
- It must stick to the business at hand.

When you use familiar, easy-to-understand words, your customer readily follows you and grasps your message. If your language is full of tongue-twisting technical terms, your customer may be impressed, but he may also be lost. Generally, customers or prospects are reluctant to stop a salesman and ask what a term or word means. They may not want to expose their ignorance, or they may not ask because they don't want to interrupt. In any case, if they do not uderstand you, you will be fighting an uphill battle. The customer wants to understand. It is the salesman's responsibility to be sure that he does. Don't use phrases and expressions that are beneath your customer's intelligence. Do use familiar words that readily get your message across, words that create desire and close sales.

Timothy Coleman's company, a large distributor of household appliances, as well as the manufacturer of a coffee maker, was conducting a contest among its sales force. First prize was a ten day expense-paid trip to Hawaii. Tim wanted that trip for himself and his young wife. He was knocking himself out and still was no closer than third place. His wife wanted that trip, of course. One weekend with two weeks to go on the contest, she said to Tim, "Sell me a coffee pot."

Tim was delighted. He went into his presentation with candor and enthusiasm. He explained that the coffee maker offered a new concept in brewing coffee; that it was, in fact, an indispensable appliance. It was decorative as well as functional. It featured the latest electronic advances and was precisely engineered. It had professional design. The beautiful appliance was as modern as space-age technology could make it—Here his wife stopped him.

"Does it make good coffee?" she asked.

Tim stopped in amazement. He got the point. Next week the gist of his sales presentation was this, as he showed his coffee maker to each customer:

"This unit makes delicious coffee. Once your customer tries it she will never want to be without it. And she will tell her friends about it. Let's make a pot. It takes only five minutes. I have everything we need right here."

At the end of the week Tim had moved up to second place. The following week he went over the top and took his bright wife to Hawaii.

You will note that Tim used a fast action-low vocabulary presentation to win. This technique is effective for any salesman selling any product. It creates strong desire and closes sales. It will win for you.

HOW TO CLOSE SALES WITH AN ECONOMY OF WORDS

To close sales with an economy of words is a fast action way to work. An economy of words suggests eliminating the blubber and the gingerbread from your business vocabulary. It means simple, straightforward speech aimed at a closed sale.

J.C. Dyvelle started an insurance agency specializing in major medical coverage. He is an expert salesman, and his first year's commissions amounted to $22,000 on major medical alone. But, being an expert, J.C. wasn't satisfied to settle for a figure he was sure he could beat. So he sat down to analyze his presentation and to examine his successes and failures. Here's what he discovered.

J.C. was a hard worker, but he found he was working some words too hard. In making his presentation he called attention to "elaborate and expensive" charts to prove his point. He spoke of "frightening figures and escalating inflationary costs." "Hospital care was exorbitant." Then there was the "tremendous extra burden" of the cost of anesthesia, the "horrendous" surgeon's fees, and the hospital's "rigid insistence on prompt payment."

He decided that his presentation was loaded with fat scary words that had the wrong effect. In many cases his elaborate language made the prospect feel that there was no way he could cope with the horror

J.C.'s scholarly presentation projected. In this setting the prospect wouldn't buy.

J.C. determined to simplify his sales story. He picked a simple, honest phrase as the cornerstone of his new presentation. He is still using it today. It is, "If you are sick or hurt you won't be wiped out when you have this protection."

The first year that he used this simple-worded approach, J.C.'s major medical sales jumped 55% over the previous year. Now he has two salesmen helping him. His personal income is $80,000 to $90,000 annually. This professional salesman continues to use the fast action-low vocabulary technique with every product he offers. It works to close more sales on all of them. J.C. isn't greedy. He urges every salesman to adopt the fast action-low vocabulary technique. He knows that it works.

My manufacturer's representative agency specializes in selling carpet. Experienced carpet salesmen know about fourth and fifth generation yarns, up-twisted denier, plys, tak gum resist dyeing, tuft bind, flame spread ratings, smoke density, fuel contribution, double jute thermoplastic bonded back, built-in super-foam pad, etc. Too, we could say that our carpet comes in a responsive range of fashions and colors, has different moods, differs from pattern to pattern, from color to color, and intermingles beautifully from style to style.

Yes, we could say all this to a wholesaler or dealer, but we wouldn't close many sales. Instead, we speak of color, texture and value as we use our samples to back up our economy of words. It works. Last year our top man had over $1,500,000 in personal production. This year the top man will hit $2,000,000 or more at his present rate of closed sales.

An economy of words can produce an abundance of business. The trick is to use fast-action, low-vocabulary words.

BEWARE KILLER WORDS

As you work to perfect your fast-action, low-vocabulary closing technique, beware killer words. Killer words are words that go nowhere and say nothing. They lack muscle and have no sales closing power. They deal in generalities. It takes specifics to close sales—words that describe, inspire, motivate, and create desire.

Listed below are enough killer words to enable you to recognize and discard any that are akin to them. Note how little such words truly say about any product or proposal.

Great	Amazing	Wonderful
Nice	Lovely	Best
Cozy	World beater	Sweet deal
Pleasing	Supreme	Miraculous
Marvelous	Darling	Cute
Very	Cheap	Hot number

You know that it is a fact of life that your customer or prospect's primary interest is what you, your product, or your proposal can do for him. Before you can close your sale your words are going to have to convince him that he will benefit from doing business with you. If you say your product is "nice," for example, he may nod in agreement, but will be thinking "so what!" If you say your proposal is "great," the same thing will happen. Killer words do not create excitement or close sales because they do not explain how and why the customer will benefit. All they will do is produce a ho-hum and so-what attitude.

By contrast, there are mind-opener words that fit into the fast-action, low-vocabulary category. They are not big fat words. They are working words that pack a wallop. Here are enough examples of such potent words to stir your imagination. Use these to uncover other fast-action, low-vocabulary words which will speed the closing of your sales.

Value	Proof	Winner
Dominant	Leader	Safe
You	Profit	We
Now	Turnover	Margin
Traffic	Cost control	Savings
Foolproof	Efficient	Decreased overhead
Ready	Security	New
Promotional	Good buy	Money
Bargain		Tested

Such words as the above are direct, easy to understand, and to the point. Use them without icing or garnish. You don't get paid for flowery speeches. You get paid for the sales you close. The fast-action, low-vocabulary route is a no-nonsense closing method.

TOM FIELD'S CONFUSION INDEX

Tom Field sells for a multi-operations electronics firm. There is a world of technical language that you can toss at a buyer in that ever-changing business. Tom never earned over $15,000 any year until he woke up to the fact that he was boring and confusing people with too much supposedly impressive technical lingo. Tom says he sounded more like a service engineer than a salesman in those days.

This quick-witted salesman decided to streamline his sales talk into a fast-action, low-vocabulary pattern. He cut out most of the words that did little besides show that he was acquainted with them. He replaced them with short words such as we have been discussing—words with zip and power to close.

Another thing Tom did to keep his closing vocabulary on target was to work up a "Confusion Index." He uses this index to keep on target as he moves in for the closed sale. His "Confusion Index" tells Tom when his customer is becoming bored or confused. It consists of questions that jolt Tom back into the language of the fast closer. Here it is:

CONFUSION INDEX (As Prepared by Tom Field)

- **Does my customer look puzzled?**
- **Am I annoying my customer with unfamiliar words?**
- **Does my customer ask me to repeat my sales points?**
- **Can my customer understand how and why my product works better than the competition's?**
- **Is my customer showing signs of boredom?**
- **Does my customer keep backing off?**
- **Is my customer's attention straying?**
- **Is my customer interested, but hesitant?**
- **Has my customer asked me to "speed it up?"**
- **Is my customer listening with only one ear?**

When the answer is "yes" to any of these questions Tom pulls up and falls back on shorter, fast action words. His income has risen to over $50,000 annually. He's thinking about renaming his confusion index "The $50,000 Confusion Index." Tom says it's worth that and more to him.

Chart your own index. Commit it to memory, as Tom does. Anything that keeps your fast-action, low-vocabulary technique closing sales is worth money to you.

The way to prepare your personal chart, or index, to avoid confusing the customer and losing the sale is this:

Check your sales presentation for killer words first of all. Take out the ones that say nothing to help close the sale. Next, remove the smart-sounding technical, or professional, terms which may go over your customer's head. Then prepare a list constructed around the Tom Field Confusion Index. Use it to catch warning signals during your presentation, as Tom does. Memorize the points on your list until you automatically watch for the danger signals. You will value your personal "Confusion Index" as Tom does. It will help you close sales.

HOW TO STICK WITH FAST ACTION WORDS
THAT CLOSE THE SALE

There is sometimes stress and pressure involved in closing a sale. The man who has never felt this strain hasn't closed many sales. Under the weight of the give and take of an important business transaction it is possible for the experienced salesman to be thrown off balance. The major danger is that he may be temporarily side-tracked from his fast-action, low-vocabulary manner of speech. Fortunately, the skilled and experienced salesman anticipates such times and will be prepared to deal with the hazard. Here are proven techniques you can employ to insure that you stick with fast action words that close your sale.

Stay in control of your presentation. Don't be drawn into a flurry of conversation that has nothing to do with closing the sale. If your customer asks technical questions, give him technical answers—if they will help close your sale. Otherwise, bring him back to the business at hand with your own rehearsed fire-cracker words. Above all, don't fall into the trap of trying to win a big word argument. You may prove you have the more sophisticated vocabulary, but your customer or prospect may feel a great compulsion to show that you can't close the sale.

It is, of course, important that you know what you are going to say before you come eyeball to eyeball with your customer. Select your most potent words and phrases and rehearse how you will use them on each customer. This doesn't mean staying up until the wee hours every night. It does mean that if a man is worth calling on, then it is worth your time to plan and practice the fast action vocabulary you will use to close your sale. When you are thus prepared you can close as planned despite any irritations that might arise.

Here are questions that will enable you to check how well you are sticking to your fast action words as you put your fast-action, low-vocabulary technique to work. Look back on your last sales call and ask yourself:

- Did I get off to a fast action start?
- Did I grab and hold my customer's attention?

- Did I stay within the language limitations of my customer?
- Was my speech friendly as well as business-like?
- Did I stick to my chosen fast action words?
- Did I resist the temptation to inject unnecessary technical terms into my presentation?
- Did my words come naturally and convincingly?
- Was I careful not to talk down to my customer?

If your sale was closed you know you are on the right track. If not, use these questions to keep on target with your fast-action, low-vocabulary closing power.

PURVES' INSTANT POINTERS ON HOW TO USE THE FAST-ACTION, LOW-VOCABULARY TECHNIQUE TO CLOSE

- **Words are the special tools of the salesman.**
- **The winner works with fast-action, low-vocabulary words.**
- **The fast-action, low-vocabulary closing technique consists of strong, working words that create desire.**
- **The fast-action, low-vocabulary method lets you close with an economy of words.**
- **Beware killer words. They have no place in your fast-action, low-vocabulary closing presentation.**
- **You avoid confusion with the fast-action, low-vocabulary process.**
- **Stick with fast-action words by practicing and controlling your fast-action, low-vocabulary closing.**
- **Periodic self-analysis is an important sales tool. Ask yourself closing questions to give your fast-action, low-vocabulary the power and intensity of a blowtorch.**

14

How to Close by Talking Profit

Walter Rathenac, a German executive and leader, once made a statement that sharply defines the salesman's role in all his business activities. He suggested that the word profit should be replaced with the word responsibility. Clearly, it is the salesman's responsibility to enhance his customer's profit structure. The salesman has an obligation to understand profit. It is his inherent duty to help improve his customer's profit performance—to help his customer make more money. The better he discharges this responsibility, the more sales he will close.

The current connotation given profit by some misguided people is lamentable. Some quarters strive to attach a stigma to profit. To put this attitude in focus, suppose, just suppose, that a company could operate without a profit. Who would meet its payroll? Who would pay the rent? This company could pay no taxes, make no social contributions, nor could it hope to expand its goods and services. It could not contribute to the support of our government, our schools, or our hospitals. In fact, without profit it would most likely be dependent upon your tax dollars in order to exist. Would you want to work for such a company? Indeed, would you consider a selling (or any other) career that could not offer you a profit in one form or another? I think not.

To drive home the salesman's overriding responsibility in this matter of profit, let's pose another question. What good is a bankrupt customer or prospect? How many sales could you expect to close in this dismal environment?

HOW TO USE PROFIT AS THE GREAT MOTIVATOR

Money gain—profit—is a great motivator to put to work in closing a sale. In today's society the importance of money is evident to everyone.

It may be true, as someone has said, that money won't buy happiness. Be that as it may, it does keep the wheels turning, and it fosters many good things. It is the badge of the successful businessman. It has a powerful appeal to anyone that you may call on. Use it as a basic closing tool.

Money may not be considered an outright emotional appeal. However, when you direct your customer's attention to what he can buy with the money you help him make or save, you have a potent emotional appeal. Satisfying your customer's wants or needs with the extra profit you can help him generate is one way to close a sale.

Closing by talking profit can be divided into two parts: (1) using the appeal of money that you can help your customer make, and (2) using the appeal of the money you can save him.

Your larger, more aggressive customers will be interested in the money that you can help them make. They are businessmen, men of vision and action. The idea of added profit excites them. When you show your customer or prospect in this group how you can help him make more money you can close your sale.

Joe Dehaven, a stockholder and just about the total marketing division of a small but enterprising food processor, had been working for over a year to get started with the biggest food distributor in his area. The answer had always been a polite, "but we have never handled anything but well-known brands."

Now Joe had a bright idea. He put his proposal in writing. Based on his knowledge of the distributor's volume, he knew that 2000 cases of green beans per month was a conservative figure. He proposed to sell a private label to the wholesale distributor—their own label—at fifty cents a case less than their leading brand. Joe's proposition showed that Afton Foods would make an extra $1000 every month with the private label program he proposed, plus an equal amount that could be picked up because of their stronger competitive position.

Joe closed his sale when he used profit as the great motivator to get his customer off dead center. His firm also profited since there was a dollar a case margin involved for his company.

Earl Deboy talked profit with a chain of supermarkets and won himself a pay increase of one hundred dollars per week. Here's how he did it:

Earl Deboy was a salesman for a leading candy and tobacco wholesaler in the Midwest. He called on Dollards Supermarkets, a multi-store chain, and regularly took care of their tobacco requirements. Earl was well aware of the great volume of candy Dollards sold, but he also realized that his firm could not handle all their candy business. Earl's company was large, but warehouse space was at a premium and it was impossible to stock all of Dollards' requirements until such a time as Midwest Promotion, Inc., Earl's employer, could expand its facilities. However, Earl figured he could stock and service single bar candy and gum racks at Dollards' check-out counters. This would mean extra profit for Dollards and for Midwest Promotions. Earl did his homework by gathering data from leading supermarket and chain store publications. When he had his facts and figures organized he was ready to use profit as the great motivator. The figures he had compiled were convincing evidence of the extra profit candy racks at check-out counters would produce for Dollards. Earl made an appointment and met with Dollards' buying committee. The following week he had a phone call confirming that Dollards had bought his idea and was ready to go.

Earl had closed his sale by talking profit. His firm promptly showed its appreciation by giving Earl a one hundred dollar per week raise and making him a supervisor in charge of all supermarket activities.

Some of your accounts and prospects will be the overly conservative type. They are not as adventuresome and aggressive as the men who think primarily in terms of making more money. With this category you can still close your sale by using profit as the great motivator. You must show them how much they can gain by the savings you can help them effect.

Bernard Holman works for Home-Dec, a manufacturer of end tables, commodes, and decorative accessories for the home. He tells about a customer who had three prosperous stores, but always bought minimal shipments from a competitor. Bernie captured the account with a trailer load order. He did this by offering his firm's usual truck load discounts and pointing out the freight savings his offer would effect. Since the stores were located in adjacent cities, Bernie could arrange for the trailer load to be split into three drop-offs.

The competition couldn't believe that Bernie had sold a trailer load in one order to this tight-fisted dealer. But Bernie's $1000 commission on this order was ironclad proof that profit made by *saving* the customer money is a valid closing technique. In passing, it is well to note that Bernie still sells this customer—and never less than a trailer load at a time.

Don Starkes took advantage of this savings technique to close a $200,000 key man insurance sale. His friend, Martin Chappel, president of a plastics concern, objected that the term insurance proposal which Don recommended was simply spending money. So Don came back with a proposal for $200,000 whole life. He pointed out and emphasized that the accumulated dividends and cash value of this policy represented savings as well as key man protection. Naturally, the premium was much higher than term insurance. But the savings feature did the trick. Don closed his sale and collected the fatter commission of $6000 on the whole life policy. Mr. Chappel considered the savings feature of Don's proposal a profitable asset. Obviously, Don used profit as the great motivator. It was a wise move—if you like money.

Keep in mind that money gain—profit—in whatever form is the appeal most widely used by salesmen everywhere. You can use it as your great motivator and close more than your share of sales. And that is a thought full of profit for any experienced and aggressive salesman.

HOW TO TELL PROFIT STORIES
THAT CLOSE THE SALE

Case histories are solid evidence that can back up your profit stories. When you have a Doubting Thomas on your hands, tell him a profit story, a true story relating the profit that your products and ideas have helped other dealers, customers, or clients, realize. You can show him invoice copies, newspaper ads, bills of lading copies, and other tangible evidence of profitable activity in his area. A word of caution: use discretion as you employ this technique. Do not do or say anything that would give away your customer's trade secrets, or damage him in any manner, as you use case histories to close your sale with the recalcitrant man you are eye-balling. It has been my experience that the customers and friends whom you have helped make money will gladly repay the favor by verifying your stories for you. In fact, I have urged a questioning buyer to pick up the phone and call the source of more than one of my profit stories right on the spot. I have invariably received the support I needed. And I've always been careful to pay for the phone call myself.

Martin Graham sells a leading upholstery-cleaning unit. It is one of the types utilizing the newest methods. This machine is designed for professionals, but it is so easy to operate that housewives and others can use it too. Martin offers a package deal with all the necessary cleaning materials and complete instructions. The units are available on a rental or a lease basis as well as outright purchase. Martin has had outstanding success with this program. He tells a lot of profit stories that he can back up as he continues his amazing record of closed sales today.

Recently Martin made his third call on the most enterprising wholesaler in his area. He had, of course, already determined that he had a tough nut to crack. This time he brought in facts and figures on three other out-of-state wholesalers. The figures showed how many units each had bought and the profit realized by these firms. On each work sheet was the buyer's name and phone number.

On this trip Martin asked Stewart Olenhouse, buyer for Three State Supply, to verify what he (Martin) had been saying all along about the profit to be had in handling his machine. He gave Mr. Olenhouse the three sheets with figures, profit projections, and the buyers' phone numbers.

Olenhouse made one call then turned and said, "That's good enough for me! How soon can we get delivery on our first order?"

Martin wrote a rush order as soon as Mr. Olenhouse gave him the P.O. number. He phoned the order to his office and collected his $500 commission the following month. That was only the beginning. Martin is still reaping commissions from this account because he closed his first sale with a convincing profit story.

Any experienced salesman has a hatful of profit stories that will excite a hesitant buyer. Don't let yours go to waste. They will close sales and make your job more profitable as well as add to your grateful customer's profit sheet.

HOW TO CLOSE ON YOUR OWN PROFIT CONTRIBUTION

Customers and buyers in every kind of business recognize a competent and efficient salesman as a real contributor to their profit picture. Who else brings them so many ideas? Who else introduces so many new products to them? Who else offers so much expertise in training personnel and helping to move goods as does the conscientious salesman? Who else helps a busy customer keep abreast of what is new and profitable in his field? The answer is, of course, only the salesman. A good salesman can help make a profitable business more profitable. A good salesman can help a struggling business to become profitable. A good salesman can close sales on the strength of his profit contribution. Here's how:

- If you are selling retailers, discuss the low cost and generous mark-up your item offers. When the retailer recognizes the initial profit, then point out the added profit you will contribute by helping to arrange displays and by watching his shelf stock closely. This saves him considerable in-store selling cost and thereby increases his profit through the extra savings your help contributes.

Roy Dresser, an independent manufacturer's sales agent, closed a sale for a truck load of housewares when he threw in extra profit for his customer. He did this by agreeing to work a gondola display on the first day of the anniversary sale of Markers Hardware and Home. This personal contribution Roy made to his customer's profit resulted in repeat business and added $2000 per year to his income.

It is well to note in passing that Markers' sale was held on a Saturday. This dedicated salesman stayed away from home an extra day to make a profit contribution to his customer. Roy is smart enough to know how much his personal profit contribution adds to his closed sales-to-calls ratio. Your own profit contribution is a valuable closing technique. Exploit it fully just as Roy Dresser does.

- If you are working with wholesalers and manufacturers the basics of closing on your own profit contributions remain the same. Wholesalers and manufacturers must be profit conscious. They have big investments and substantial operating costs. Every dollar of profit that you can contribute to these people is not only appreciated, but necessary. They expect nothing less of the high caliber salesmen who walk through their doors.

You can close on your own profit contribution with this profit-conscious clientele by emphasizing the quality, price and ready availability of your line. Too, you can help such firms control inventory and thus make a profit contribution. You can be sure that their stocks are balanced and that needed goods are always in stock. In order to profit, these firms require good quality, a fair price, and a ready source of supply for prompt delivery. When you illustrate your qualifications to meet these requirements, you make a profit contribution that is readily recognizable and one that will close your sale.

Tommy Sissel closed on his own profit contribution when he arranged for weekly deliveries to a wholesaler friend who was cramped for space due to growing pains. Tommy sells frozen foods. Midstate Foods, Tommy's wholesaler friend, had added a large freezer room, but it quickly proved to be inadequate. Midstate's old supplier could deliver certain institutional foods only twice a month. As a result

Midstate Foods was often out of important items. The second week Tommy had learned of this problem. First, he talked with his office to be sure of his ground. Then he laid the weekly delivery proposition before Midstate Foods—with the added proviso that emergency deliveries could be made. Tommy didn't have to belabor the profit idea. Midstate Foods knew that Tommy was making a real profit contribution. The deal was closed. Today Midstate Foods have larger facilities and Tommy's company still helps them add to their profit structure. But Tommy doesn't call on them every week anymore. He can't. He's too busy directing the sales force of the food processing concern he works for. The board of directors have even bigger plans for Tommy. Making a personal profit contribution to close a sale *is* a way for an ambitious man to get ahead.

Mike Strab earned a $1500 commission when he made his profit contribution to a wood products firm. Mike noted on his first call that Starr Wood Products was behind the times on their load handling equipment. Fork lifts were used, to be sure. But Mike had ready figures showing that much overtime would be eliminated and that a savings of $9000 annually would be effected with his Super Truck. This truck could lift 6-ton loads on a platform bed. It had the capacity to reach second story levels and could smoothly stockpile lumber to efficient storage heights. Further, it could be converted to other uses, such as a dump truck.

Mike closed his sale on the second call with this fistful of proof that he could add to his customer's profit. This observant salesman says that making a personal profit contribution is the best way he knows to close a sale.

HOW TO CLOSE BY DEMONSTRATING PROFITABILITY

To demonstrate is to prove. When proof is offered of an item or an idea's profitability, the closing of the sale is at hand. One of the simple and convincing ways to demonstrate profitability is to put it in writing. When you do this your customer can see as well as hear what you are saying. Here is an example.

There are variables in figuring profit per square foot for a retailer. The problem is that some retailers take aisle space and storage space into account. For our purposes, we will demonstrate the profit by considering the profit per square foot of the display space your merchandise will occupy.

To illustrate let's assume a unit of your merchandise takes up one square foot of space and has a mark-up (gross profit) of ten dollars. Obviously, this is ten dollars profit per square foot. This is somewhat over-simplified, but will give you the idea.

It's not likely you will ever get exactly one square foot. Here is the formula to arrive at profit per square foot. Take the gross profit of all the merchandise displayed in your allotted space and divide it by the number of square feet. This will give you the profit per square foot.

If you have forty square feet and the profit per square foot is ten dollars, then you have a profit of four hundred dollars. If the merchandise turns ten times a year you have an annual gross profit of $4000, and so on.

It is not our purpose to get into a lot of mathematics. If you need to sharpen your skills in this department there are other reference sources. Our purpose is to stir up ideas in your own thinking which will enable you to close more sales by demonstrating profitability. Retailers, wholesalers, and anybody else who handles merchandise for resale will always be ready to do business with the salesman who can demonstrate profitability on the above basis.

Not all profit is figured per square foot. To wit, when you demonstrate a savings you are demonstrating profitability that closes sales.

Earlier in this chapter we discussed how to tell profit stories that close the sale. This is another method of demonstrating profitability. Don't overlook this technique. It is a proven, field-tested way to close by demonstrating profitability.

Morton Presnor, who sold shelf items to just about everybody west of the Mississippi until his recent retirement, carried a set of charts illustrating profitability on every item he sold. These charts also showed projected turnover on each item. Old Mort maintained that these charts saved a lot of time when he was demonstrating profitability. They closed a lot of sales, too, for Mort seldom paid income taxes on less that $100,000 per year.

PURVES' INSTANT POINTERS ON HOW TO CLOSE
BY TALKING PROFIT

- **Profit: The salesman's responsibility.**
- **What good is a bankrupt customer?**
- **Profit is the great motivator.**

- Profit is the most widely used closing appeal employed by experienced salesmen.
- Case histories back up profit stories that close sales.
- You can close sales on the basis of your own personal profit contribution.
- When you demonstrate profitability the closing of your sale is at hand.

15

How to Close
with Fringe Benefits

Fringe benefits are akin to wants. Like wants they are often a more powerful closing tool than raw needs.

Today's society is tuned and conditioned to expect fringe benefits. Fringe benefits are that something extra, that something free, that the buyer gets along with the goods or services his money buys. Fringe benefits are cherished. They stand out in the mind of the buyer over and above cost. These additional benefits often can and do supersede cold logic in the buying process. They pack an emotional wallop that closes sale after sale.

It is easy to understand the force and appeal of fringe benefits. Your wife cooks your dinner and looks after your home, but it is her kisses and love that binds you to her. Her utility is recognized and appreciated. However, she knows and you know that it is the comfort and warm companionship—the fringe benefits—which she embodies that keeps you coming home to her.

The principle of fringe benefits works the same way in closing a sale. You must use your product knowledge and your strong sales personality to make clear to the customer or prospect the utility and concrete advantages of your goods, ideas, or services. When you have done this that is the time to heap the goodies on top of it all. Your sound sales presentation will give him the logical reasons to buy. The fringe benefits, the extra added benefit you can offer free of cost, can tip the scales in your favor.

Use fringe benefits for one purpose only, to close your sale fast. Do not throw them in the air like a handful of confetti as little conversational pieces. Of course, you want your customer to think of you as a nice, friendly guy who is a good talker. Nonetheless, you are more than a conversationalist—you are a salesman, a businessman, intent on getting the job done. As such, use fringe benefits in the only way that will help you and your customer. Close your sale with them. Both you and your customer will then have the added benefits that accrue from this professional handling of this powerful closing appeal.

HOW TO USE "PRIDE OF OWNERSHIP" TO CLOSE

Any time a man invests his money in something, he wants to feel that he has done the smart thing. He wants to be proud of what he has bought, whether it is a ten dollar necktie or a ten million dollar yacht. The salesman who makes the most of the pride of ownership appeal is going to close more sales.

A suit priced at $125 will keep a man warm, but a $300 suit makes him proud. The salesman selling high quality clothing knows the fringe benefit he is offering. It's called pride of ownership, and the salesman closes many extra sales on this basis. A salesman I first bought a suit from over twenty-five years ago put it this way, "Sure, this suit costs three hundred dollars, but for less than one dollar a day you will be wearing a suit that you are proud to own. A cheaper suit will keep you comfortable, but it can't give you anything extra."

My friend refuses to work any way other than on a straight commission basis. His reasoning is sound. His boss has confided to me that there have been months when this knowledgeable salesman has closed so many sales that he has made more money than the boss himself. His favorite closing technique was and still is the pride of ownership appeal

A retired army officer moved to our town a few years ago. He wanted to buy a house. This man was accustomed to making decisions and giving orders. The retired colonel made it plain that he wanted a house in a desirable area and, furthermore, that he would not pay a penny over $50,000 for it. After this red hot prospect had worn out three other real estate agents with his uncompromising attitude, Bert Schann, salesman for Brentmoor Homes, inherited him. During the rather hectic qualifying interview, Bert found that his prospect liked trees and wanted a house with a view. After this brief interview Bert rose and said, "Come on. Colonel, I have just the house for you!"

Bert took his client to see a well-built three-bedroom house on an expansive lot just outside the city limits. There were eight large trees in the yard. They could see from the front a panoramic view of the James River and its lush valley. "How much?" asked the Colonel.

"Sixty thousand dollars," answered Bert.

"I guess you didn't hear me," growled the army man. "I said $50,000 was the limit."

"Okay," Bert said, "Let's go look at some $50,000 homes, I wanted you to see this place first though. As we agreed, it's a beautiful house with all those majestic trees and a gorgeous view. It would make a home you and your wife would be proud to own and proud to show your friends."

All day long Bert and the Colonel looked at houses in the $50,000 range. When night came Bert took the Colonel back to his office and they said goodnight.

The next morning as Bert was checking new listings to show the Colonel, his phone rang. "I've decided to buy that first house you showed me, Mr. Schann," the Colonel abruptly stated.

Of course, Bert lost no time in closing the deal. True, he had bought a lovely home. But Bert had sold him pride of ownership rather than a house. This is a closing technique that works on everything from hot air balloons to land sales.

Alan Rovine sells typewriters. He uses pride of ownership to sell his most highly developed electronic model. His closing statement usually goes like this: "Here's a machine you will be proud to own and that your secretary will be proud to use."

Last month Alan sold one of his most expensive models to a small three-man office with this appeal. The volume of correspondence going out of that office isn't all that great, but the pride of ownership more than justifies the electronic typewriter. It works the same in businesses large and small when you use this fringe benefit to close.

HOW TO CLOSE WITH THE "PRESTIGE APPEAL"

Prestige is something we all covet. Prestige means standing or estimation in the eyes of people, a commanding position in men's minds. What our peers think of us is important to us. This appeal ties in with the pride of ownership appeal in that it is a powerful closing tool appealing to men's pride.

A contractor sold the president of a small firm a complete and larger building by using the prestige appeal. W.C. Murphy was proud of the volume of business his small firm did in the compact building he had used for ten years. John Chrysler, the aggressive contractor-salesman, was aware of this. He also knew that sooner or later somebody would build a new plant for the Murphy Company. So he drew up a preliminary set of plans and made an appointment with Mr. Murphy. Mr. Murphy's reaction was, as expected. "But we're doing all right in this building."

At this point John Chrysler said, "Mr. Murphy, you're a man of esteem in business and in the community as a whole. You are looked upon as a successful man. I'm wondering, though, if you know that some of your customers doing less business than you do operate out of bigger facilities that you have? Larger, more impressive quarters will not only provide room for your future growth, your prestige among your suppliers as well as your customers will be enhanced. Isn't this more than enough reason to get started on a new building at once?"

Mr. Murphy agreed. The sale was closed. John collected his $50,000 profit on the sale. He continues to use this fringe benefit to close deals and make money today. It's an idea that will close sales and make more money for any dedicated salesman.

A specialty salesman, Walter Noble, won a new account with the prestige appeal. A competitor had been selling this firm a line of goodwill calendars for a number of years. The competitor's art work was acceptable and the price per thousand had held close to 50¢ each. Walter showed a line of calendars costing $1.25 each per thousand. The art work had better detail than the competitor's and the printing was superior. Walter closed his sale by pointing out that, though his calendars cost seventy-five cents more, the added prestige would result in many dollars of additional business for his customer. The calendars alone, he explained, were a real buy. The fringe benefit of prestige was the bigger part of the bargain, Walter emphasized. The first order was for 10,000 calendars. Walter has other prestigious items he plans to sell his new friend. When you follow Walter's example and use the prestige appeal as a fringe benefit to close, you can land new customers and outsmart your competition.

HOW TO CLOSE WITH THE SECURITY BENEFIT APPEAL

Ours is a security-conscious world. This single fact leaves the gate open to close many a sale with the security benefit appeal.

Leo Krugman specializes in selling annuities. He is well acquainted with everyone's desire to be secure and independent in his old age. Leo belongs to an exclusive businessman's club in his home town. The club serves delightful meals to members and their guests. When Leo has a prize prospect for an annuity plan he invariably arranges to take his prospect to his club for lunch. This shrewd salesman purposely drives through a shabby district where winos and derelicts loaf in doorways and on the sidewalks. As he drives through this section, Leo slows his car a bit and thoughtfully observes, "I wonder where these old men would be today if they had bought an annuity years ago?"

This sobering picture of penniless old men dramatically conditions the young man riding with Leo. He is usually attentive and receptive to Leo's annuity proposal. In fact, Leo says that the security benefit appeal closes one out of every three clients he takes to lunch. This one bit of showmanship which so strikingly reinforces the security benefit appeal for Leo has propelled him into the top money bracket in his agency for five consecutive years to date.

The investment broker must often close with the security benefit appeal as well as the income and growth opportunities that his proposal may represent. People with large amounts of money do not usually care to speculate wildly with it. They like to invest it, sure, but they want to feel reasonably safe in doing so.

Howard K. Matthews works for a prominent brokerage firm in one of our large Eastern cities. He recently earned $25,000 commission by putting the security benefit appeal to work. Howard was dealing with a committee of three who were in the market for $1,500,000 of municipal bonds. These gentlemen were part of a holding company seeking sound buys and solid investments. All three men agreed that Howard's proposal had the earnings rate they sought. However, the more cautious of the three kept questioning the "security" of Howard's portfolio. Howard asked for a thirty minute appointment the next day. At the appointed time he was there with the records and testimonials of ten of his bigger clients. In each case the client's figures and recommendation supported Howard's keen judgment and verified the performance of the selections he had sold the client. Indeed, some of the very bonds Howard again had available were in the investment portfolio of two of these ten. With this assurance Howard closed his $1,500,000 sale. He had the right merchandise all along, but it took the fringe benefit of security appeal to nail down the gratifying transaction.

The security benefit appeal can be used to close sales on everything from automobile tires to saftey plate glass. You can use your experience and ability to capitalize on this universal appeal. It's a paying proposition.

HOW TO CLOSE WITH THE "LEADERSHIP" BENEFIT

People in general and business and professional people in particular like to be regarded as leaders. This appeal has moved everything from neckties to race horses. For instance:

Nathan Segal had called on a leading tobacco and sundry distributor for three months trying to close a sale on electronic data equipment. There is a lot of record keeping to be done in this type of operation and Nathan's prospective customer had eleven branch houses in addition to the headquarters house. Nathan was meticulous in explaining the operation and the advantages of his system. Yet each time he tried to close, Pete Martino the third generation president of Martino Tobacco and Sundry, merely squirmed like a worm in hot ashes and murmured something to the effect that, "We've been getting along pretty well without that stuff for nearly four generations."

On this trip Nathan was ready and closed his deal with the leadership benefit appeal. Here's how:

Mr. Martino: "But we've been getting along pretty well without that fancy stuff for nearly four generations."

Nathan Segal: "Yes, Mr. Martino, you certainly have. For nearly eighty years your family has been a leader in your industry. You are recognized for being aggressive and a man who sets the pace. I noticed three new delivery vans and a large tractor trailer unit on your lot last night. Now, your grandfather used horses and wagons when he started, didn't he? You couldn't operate that way today, could you, Mr. Martino?"

Mr. Martino: "Obviously not."

Nathan Segal: "Okay, consider this. Your record keeping apparatus is still about the same today as in the beginning, isn't it? Oh, you do have a few new office machines, but basically, it hasn't changed much, has it?"

Mr. Martino: "I guess not."

Nathan Segal: "Well, I'm sure you want your son to continue your fine tradition of leadership. Would it be fair to hand such an ambitious young man an outmoded system? Wouldn't this hamper him and the whole corporation in the constant race to be the leader? You've done everything else to equip him to be a front runner. You owe this modern high-speed data processing system to your son and to your business if you want this respected firm to stay out front. I've given you every speck of information on the system. Your chief competitor has had it for ten years. Don't you think we should insure your leadership position by arranging for the installation of this equipment now?"

Mr. Martino, after a long, thoughtful pause: "Could we begin putting it in next week?

Nathan collected his $3000 when he was handed his next check. Mr. Martino is still proudly boasting of his outstanding leadership position and his up-to-date electronic record keeping system. Both men are the envy of their peers.

This desire for leadership (leadership benefit) is nothing of which to be ashamed. Without this inherent urge mankind would wallow in mediocrity, salesmen would fail, and businesses fold. It is strong medicine. Use it to close big sales, just as Nathan Segal does today.

DON'T BE STINGY WITH THE GOODIES

Most worthwhile sales are closed because some skilled salesman motivated a customer to make a rational, mutually profitable decision. Fringe benefits are frequently the major or most powerful reason for buying.

We have discussed a few of the most patent fringe benefit appeals. There are many others you can use to close more sales and keep you moving ahead. The following will give you an idea of the number of other fringe benefits which you can call upon to close your sale. The list is by no means complete, but it should be enough to start the wheel turning.

Comfort	Education	Health
Sex	Ego	Love
Respect	Style	Recreation
Beauty	Safety	Sentiment
Pleasure	Status	Success
Attention	Self-esteem	Power
Romance	Popularity	Imitation
Emulation (keeping up with the Joneses)		Achievement

It is good closing strategy to choose the fringe benefit appeal that will help you close your sale even as your organize all the concrete reasons why your customer should buy. This way you have both barrels loaded as you take aim on your closed sale. There are far too many fringe benefits to list for every product or service and every selling situation. Don't be stingy with these goodies. They often close sales where sheer logic and sound reason must take a back seat.

YOU GET FRINGE BENEFITS ALSO

It naturally follows that you get fringe benefits also when you employ the fringe benefits appeal. Here are a few that you can expect.

- You close sales that otherwise would fall by the wayside.
- You tie your customer closer to you by giving him an important something extra.
- Your closing skill grows and expands as you become more efficient in recognizing and applying the force and the charm of fringe benefits.
- Combining logic and the fringe benefits appeal gives you SOP— Standard Operating Procedure—to close more sales.
- You make more money.

PURVES' INSTANT POINTERS ON HOW TO CLOSE WITH FRINGE BENEFITS

- Today's society is conditioned to expect fringe benefits.
- Use fringe benefits to close your sale fast.
- The salesman who makes the most of the "Pride of Ownership Appeal" is going to close more sales.
- Like the "Pride of Ownership Appeal," the "Prestige Appeal" is a powerful closing tool.
- Ours is a security-conscious world. This leaves the gate open to close sales with the "Security Benefit Appeal."
- The "Leadership Benefit" is strong medicine.
- Don't be stingy with the goodies.
- You get fringe benefits also.

16

How to Close When the Prospect Can't Make Up His Mind

It's a frustrating undertaking to deal on any level with the individual who cannot make up his mind. It is equally, or more frustrating, to work with a committee that goes back and forth like the tide. Yet this is exactly the position a hard-working, conscientious salesman sometimes finds himself in as he struggles to close his sale. It is not the ideal atmosphere in which to close a sale. But it can be done.

One thing that a salesman must keep in mind when he faces the indecisive customer or prospect is that he, the salesman, is probably more comfortable than the poor soul who can't make up his mind to do what he knows he ought to do. As we have noted before, decision making can be an excruciating experience for some. To close his sale, the salesman must take the pain out of the decision-making process for this type. In fact, this species is usually waiting for the salesman to make up his mind for him. When the salesman does this by exercising logic, fairness, and good business sense, he creates a loyal customer. Mr. Indecision is looking for the man who can relieve him of the burden of making up his mind, and who can help him make money and prosper as he does so. Fit yourself into this picture and you can close sale after sale with the customer or prospect who agonizes over decision making. Make up your mind to do just that.

MAKE A HERO OF THE WISHY-WASHY TYPE

The wishy-washy customer who can't make up his mind is usually frightfully insecure. He is afraid to decide yes and he is afraid to decide no. Consequently, he stalls and waits, even though making no decision could be the worst decision of all. This type requires a double dose of reassurance. When you can show him that he is on solid ground in dealing with you, you are home free. Make a hero of the wishy-washy buyer and you can practically write your own ticket.

Richard Arnall, a St. Louis salesman with a line of rubber footwear, was always sure of an order from McGregan Bros. Inc., a wholesaler of dry goods, shoes, and notions. When Richard called with his Fall Campaign Promotions he always knew Mr. Stump, the aging buyer, would place an order for $5,000 and not a penny more. This had been going on for several years. Mr. Stump was proud of his fast "turnover." His prideful boast every time he had to call in a rush fill-in order was, "We sold out again!"

The obvious problem was that he never took note of the many scratch-outs and lost sales his timidity caused. Of course, Richard had urged him to buy adequate stocks, but that called for a new decision and a bit of new thinking. Besides, Mr. Stump reasoned, he always sold out of the $5,000 order.

It goes without saying that the sales force complained about the business they lost because Mr. Stump could not decide to do what he knew he should do. It was a sad situation and Richard knew that it was up to him to turn it around.

When Richard's next fall and winter promotion on rubber footwear was ready, he worked up an order five times as big as the customary $5,000 order. His proposal included boots and styles Mr. Stump had never ordered, but merchandise Richard knew would sell.

Richard spread the proposed order before Mr. Stump and said, "Here's what we're going to do this fall. We are going to ship this as a minimum first order, Mr. Stump. We are all going to make some money on this line this year — your company, your salesmen, and me. Your past purchase records prove that $25,000 is a modest order for this concern. You owe it to your company, to the sales force, and to me to make this change in your old buying pattern. It's time for a positive decision. There is practically no risk involved, as your files will show."

"The boss will kill me," wavered Mr. Stump.

"No," Richard said, "he won't. He will applaud and you will be a hero to your company's salesmen. They will tell your boss about the extra business you made possible, and I will be here to point that out to him myself. Sign the order. This is not an overwhelming decision for a man of your experience."

It took a little more prodding, but Stump did sign. Further, he did become a hero and you can bet he took full credit for his big decision. This was all right with Richard Arnall. The next year the first order was even fatter. Richard had his reward because he now is earning an override of $25,000 yearly on the McGregan Bros. account. This is more than his total order used to be.

Make heroes of your wishy-washy types by helping them make the right decisions. The sales you close this way could make you rich.

HOW RAY HUNTER GOT HIS BUYER OFF THE FENCE

Ray Hunter had had a customer for several years standing for his regular line of industrial paints which he normally sold in fifty-gallon drums to industrial and manufacturing supply wholesalers. His firm Harter-Bradford Chemical, Inc. had developed a new stain that had been enthusiastically received by the trade. Reorders were rolling in at such a pace that Harter-Bradford was hard put to keep up with the demand. Despite this obvious proof that the product was superior in quality and performance, Ray had a problem with his old friend Austin Herd, buyer for the Arco Manufacturer's Supply. It had never been easy to introduce a new item to Mr. Herd. This time he was proving to be indecisive to the point of belligerency. He admitted that, indeed, Ray's stain was better than the one he had been buying for over ten years. Yet, he "wanted to wait" before making a change. Decision making often entails making a change, and a change can give seemingly strong and rational men a case of the hives. This was unquestionably the circumstance that Ray found as he worked to close his sale with Austin Herd. It was a one-on-one confrontation and Ray knew that if the only intelligent and reasonable decision were to be made he would have to bump his man off the fence of indecision.

As this point Ray played his ace. He politely but emphatically explained to Mr. Herd that he could no longer wait. His merchandise was hot, his company was demanding coverage in the area, and some action had to be taken. If Mr. Herd could not make up his mind that it was to his advantage to handle this new and important product then he, Ray, would be obliged to go to the manufacturers and industrialists and offer it to them on a direct basis. He stated that this was not his preference, but a decision had to be made. The new stain was much too valuable for his company to remain indifferent longer. Wouldn't Mr. Herd reconsider and place a stocking order at once?

Austin Herd did reconsider. He could see all that business slipping away from him if he forced his friend out into the field as his competitor. Too, he could imagine his superior's dismay when they discovered the reason for such a disaster had been his fence-straddling tendency. He agreed to place an order at once for a straight carload if Ray would agree to a thirty day wait before shipping. Mr. Herd explained that he would need this much time to move the merchandise he had in stock. Ray could understand this. The sale was closed just as quickly as Mr. Herd had made up his mind. Ray collected his $3750 commission. Mr. Herd received accolades from his management as this segment of the firm's business improved appreciably with Ray's new product.

Never make idle threats when you must take drastic steps to get your customer off the fence. Be sweet and reasonable, but be prepared to back up what you say. You can't close your sale by climbing on the fence with Mr. Indecision.

HOW TO CLOSE THIS TYPE WITH PROOF

Proof is reassurance. Reassurance is what the wishy-washy buyer requires in large doses. If nothing else, you must prove, as Ray Hunter did, that some form of positive action must be taken without undue delay. Business, and, for that matter, life itself is a constant round of decision making. In sales, as in all facets of life, procrastination only complicates matters and loses money. One of your basic responsibilities as a respected, knowledgeable salesman is to furnish proof based on your honest convictions that your product or proposal is valid and will perform to your customer's entire satisfaction. With such concrete evidence you can prod the sluggard into logical action and close your sale.

Jennifer Norton has an interest in a small picture frame manufacturing concern. In fact, Jennifer is a prime motivator in the company's remarkable success. She is one of three salespersons the firm employs. Jennifer not only sells picture frames, she will also personally deliver them from her panel truck when the occasion calls for it.

After six months Jennifer finally succeeded in seeing Mr. C.P. Henderson, of Butterfield and Henderson, a local chain of six discount variety stores. Like any good salesperson, Jennifer had done her homework. She knew what she was up against. Butterfield and Henderson was affiliated with a national buying group. And that is where they had been buying all their picture frames.

The sales interview started about as this businesswoman expected. Mr. Henderson explained his association with the buying group and expressed enthusiasm over the help the association offered him. In other words, it had taken over part of his role as a decision-maker, Jennifer reasoned. Jennifer, like any other seasoned business leader, was more than willing to assume her share of decision making for Mr. Henderson. She proceeded on this basis. Here is the gist of how she did the job:

Jennifer: "Mr. Henderson, together we have looked over samples of the frames we make. You've agreed that the quality, variety, and style are equal to, or better, than what you have been buying. What else do you need to know to convince you that your firm would do better with my line?"

Mr. Henderson: "Well, there is always the matter of price. You know that is one of the main attractions in group buying."

Jennifer: "Yes sir, I'm aware of that. Let's compare prices again. You will find that we are in the ball park in that area. As a matter of fact, we can save you some money because of your quantity buying for six stores. Too, we will eliminate all freight charges since your stores are close enough to our plant for us to give you prompt delivery on our own truck. That's a substantial savings in itself."

Mr. Henderson: "True. Still you are pretty new. How do I know you can be depended on to act as a reliable source."

Jennifer: "Your friend, Mr. Chadwick, has two stores in Chillicothe. He belongs to your buying association. Call him. He was one of our very first customers. He has done an outstanding job with our line and works closely with us today."

Mr. Henderson: "Well, let me go over this with Mr. Butterfield. Come back Monday morning. I think we may be able to work out something."

When Jennifer was ushered into Mr. Henderson's office the next Monday morning, Mr. Henderson smilingly handed her a stock order for each of the six stores. Jennifer had closed her sale with proof positive.

Jennifer is a minority stockholder in her company, but she is now on the board of directors. Her recognition of the importance of the decision-making process in marketing, as well as all phases of the business function, more than qualifies her for her new duties on the board.

Making the most of your understanding of decision making and supporting your convictions with proof will close sales for you. It will also put your abilities up front for all to see, just as it has for Jennifer Norton, who is still the most productive salesperson in her organization.

HOW TO MAKE THE DECISIONS FOR
THE CUSTOMER WHO CAN'T MAKE UP HIS MIND

As an aggressive, experienced salesman you can no doubt recall many instances when you have been required to make a decision for both you and your buyer friend. This is one of the most effective and least painful ways of dealing with the customer who can't make up his mind. Domination, that personal asset of all strong salesmen, which we discussed in the first chapter, must be called into play often to close your sale when dealing with the customer who can't make up his mind. This is in no way taking advantage of the situation, or of your buyer. In fact, the dominant salesman has kept more than one indecisive buyer out of trouble and, indeed, from the ranks of the unemployed. Decision making is a requisite for success. Nowhere is this more evident than in the role of the customer-buyer. Any contribution you make which enables your friend to be positive and quick in his decision making will constitute a real favor to him. Besides that, it closes your sale without the suffering and strain that is a built-in part of wallowing in a mess of unproductive indecision.

Adam Padgett, owner of Padgett Contractors and Excavators, had successfully bid on a project to clear 500 acres of rough timberland for a new resort complex in the lakes area of a Midwest state. Now his problem was that his bulldozer was shot, needed costly repairs, and was so old it was growing whiskers. For three years he had put off buying the machine he knew he needed, as he patched and scrounged to get by on his old piece of equipment. Periodically he had discussed his need with Harley Parker, salesman for Vanhoover Contracting and Excavating Supply. Harley had learned of Mr. Padgett's successful bid. He was waiting Monday morning when Adam Padgett arrived for work.

"Good morning, Adam," said Harley. "I have the order for your new dozer all filled out with the financing you indicated you would want. This machine is big enough to handle that 500 acre job and make you a lot of money on other projects for a long time. You're going to need a back-hoe, so I've arranged for that on the same order. All you have to do is sign today. I'll see that you get delivery right away."

"My Gosh," said Padgett, "can't we wait until we get inside to sign it?"

"Well,,' said Harley, "that will be OK if you don't get your key stuck in the door."

With that the wrangling and the indecision were over. Harley collected his $5750 commission and Mr. Padgett has long since paid for the equipment. As his firm continues to grow he still looks to Harley for his new equipment. Harley helps him prosper and relieves him of making some thorny decisions — which is only one of the reasons Harley has been offered some stock options by Vanhoover Contracting and Excavating Supply, Inc.

As a fire-balling salesman you are in the same posture as any other executive type. You are expected to make profitable decisions. Your firm expects you to do so, your customers want you to do so, and your success demands that you do so. Follow Harley's example and close sales that less dominant salesmen let slip away.

Carl Hooper quit the security of his job with a large printing concern and launched his own business, Hooper's Greeting Card and Novelty Distributors. He had studied the possibilities and now was ready to launch his new enterprise. His modest warehouse was stocked with cards, novelties, and racks for point-of-purchase display in a variety of outlets. He had his sights on the Big Owl Convenience Store, an all night quick-shop store. Big Owl was to be his first customer.

Carl knew Delbert Callaway as a well-meaning pussyfooter. He had squeezed a little printing business out of him a few times. Carl had decided that Big Owl could use two rack displays of his merchandise. Total cost to Big Owl would be $1500. Mark-up was 40% on this merchandise.

Carl unloaded one rack and took it in. He placed it and took in the other. As he was loading the racks with the merchandise he had decided would move fastest for Big Owl, Delbert Callaway came in.

"What's going on?" he screamed.

"I'm going to make you some extra money," said Carl. "Let me tell you about it."

Carl did tell him about it. He pointed out that the racks took only one square foot of space each, and that the merchandise carried a 40% mark-up — which was better than that of 90% of the items Big Owl sold.

There was a bit of squirming, but Carl stood his ground with his sound sales story. When Big Owl opened store number two, Carl was in before the doors opened. Obviously Delbert Callaway is happy with the decision that this dominant salesman made for him.

When you make the decision for the customer who can't make up his mind, your closed sale will be in your pocket.

EVERYBODY'S AHEAD WHEN
YOU CLOSE MR. INDECISION

It's not too difficult to see that everybody's ahead when you close Mr. Indecision. Nothing happens until a decision is made. And who could be in a better position to make an intelligent and profitable decision than the salesman? He is the man in the field every day, the man who keeps abreast of all that's new. He is also the man who knows what's worth hanging onto, as new ideas and new products compete with the old. With this background working for you, you are an indispensable asset to the customer or prospect who can't make up his mind.

One last thought: When there is no way to get the customer to make up his mind, you are probably talking to the wrong man. Check this out. Some misguided individual may try to boost his ego at your expense. He tries to sound like a buyer though he has neither the capacity nor the authority to buy.

PURVES' INSTANT POINTERS ON HOW TO CLOSE
WHEN THE PROSPECT CAN'T MAKE UP HIS MIND

- Make a hero of the wishy-washy type.
- You can't close your sale by climbing on the fence with Mr. Indecision.
- The wishy-washy buyer requires big doses of reassurance.
- You can use personal dominance to make the decision for the customer who can't make up his mind.
- Double check to be sure you are talking to the buyer when a prospect can't make up his mind.
- Everybody wins when you close Mr. Indecision.

17

How to Close by Appealing to the Prospect's Ego

Everybody has a little ego, or at least should have. Ego is a form of self-esteem. Can you imagine how much fun, or how profitable it would be, to call on a prospect or customer who had no sense of self-worth? Do you know anyone without a bit of ego who is doing much of anything worthwhile? I don't, and I do not think that you do either. Further, everybody likes to have his ego fed occasionally. Appealing to your customer's ego is one more way to close sales and generate repeat business.

In appealing to the prospect's or customer's ego you must be—as you must in all cases—absolutely sincere and honest. Flattery is not a closing tool. Flattery has the connotation of insincerity and trickery. When it is ladled on in heavy doses it will do damage to your intelligent customer's ego. He is likely to think that your estimation of him is low. He may feel that you regard him as stupid. Worse yet, he may consider you crude for trying such a tactless gambit. In any event, as a bright and conscientious salesman, you will never find it necessary to use questionable tactics to close a sale. When you close by appealing to the prospect's ego you can operate on the same high plane that you do when you employ your other closing techniques. Your customer's ego is important to him. Give it a boost and close your sale.

TAKE ADVANTAGE OF THIS: THE TOUGHER THEY ARE THE MORE THEY WANT THEIR EGO PAMPERED

The business community does have some blustery, crusty members. Usually the tough demanding individual is hiding behing this flimsy facade because he has some subconscious misgivings about his personal qualifications. He may be competent enough to handle his affairs, but for reasons only a psychiatrist could explain, he entertains some gnawing self-doubts. So he maintains an outwardly tough, often antagonistic attitude in a constant effort to convince himself and the whole world that he is truly a confident, dynamic leader. He wants to be liked, and he craves the respect of the salesman who calls on him. His tough stance is merely a defensive gesture, more often than not. This makes it a bit harder to deal with him on amicable terms than it is to deal with the less noisy class of prospects and customers. Nevertheless, the experienced executive-type salesman never self-destructs when he encounters a buyer who is plagued by a shaky ego. Instead, he wisely pampers the man's ego, thereby closes his sale and thus reaffirms that the tough customer needs and wants the help of a sensible, even-tempered salesman.

David Omar sold a sixty-two year old president of a bank a whole life insurance policy even though the banker had several paid up policies. David knew that the bank president was not heavily covered for a man of his station. David's co-workers hooted when they learned who David's prospect was. Not only was Mr. Childron sixty-two, he had the reputation of being tough and mean. Nevertheless, David had his secretary prepare a proposal. The next day he called cold turkey and succeeded in getting Mr. Childron to grant him a fifteen minute interview. David went over the proposal with Mr. Childron who kept insisting that by blankety-blank a man of his age didn't have any business buying more insurance. Here's what happened then:

David: "The only thing that I can think of that might keep you from getting it is passing the physical. Do you think you could do that now, Mr. Childron?"

Mr. Childron: "I don't know why not. I have a check-up every year and the doctor tells me I'm in excellent shape. Why, when I was a boy back home I could lift as much as any man for miles around, etc., etc."

David: "Tell you what, Mr. Childron, our doctor can examine you at ten o'clock tomorrow. It won't cost you a penny. If you pass we can put the insurance into effect the same day. Let's just see if you can do it!"

Mr. Childron (who was a splendid physical specimen for his age): "Well, okay, I'll try to make it."

Mr. Childron did make it and he did pass the physical. While the amount of insurance he bought wasn't the biggest policy David had ever written, the premium on a sixty-two year old is substantial. David's first year commission was nine hundred dollars.

David's co-workers are still amazed that David closed his sale—and with only one call. They don't know how he did it. But David knows that he did it by pampering the gruff old banker's ego. After all, it's not every sixty-two year old man who can pass a physical and get insurance at standard rates.

Follow David's example. You will close some surprising sales also.

Kenny Hartman operated the Crown Janitorial and Window Washing Company. Every Thursday morning he passed the Kilburn Jewelry store as he went to work. Invariably Mr. Kilburn would be washing the windows and sweeping the walks rain or shine. Kenny had tried to sell his services to Mr. Kilburn and had been brusquely informed that Mr. Kilburn could do the work himself. Furthermore, that he was smart enough to call Crown Janitorial if he should require their services. Nevertheless, Kenny stopped again on a Thursday morning. This time instead of talking about the advantages of his cleaning service, he took a different tack. After a cold start he reminded Mr. Kilburn that his was a prestigious business. He asked if Mr. Kilburn wouldn't agree that it would leave a better impression with Kilburn Jewelers' clientele if they did not see Mr. Kilburn washing his own windows and doing the sweeping. He suggested that Mr. Kilburn was much too important to be doing menial chores.

There were a few more minutes of blustering on Mr. Kilburn's part. However, Kenny had hit home. He had hit the hot button when he appealed to Mr. Kilburn's ego. Mr. Kilburn agreed to turn over the cleaning end of his business to Crown Janitorial. When Kenny changed his sales technique to fit the circumstances and appealed to the gentleman's ego, he closed his sale.

Take advantage of the sales closing power of the ego appeal. Pamper the ego of the tough prosect or customer. The money is good.

HOW TO FIND AND USE
HONEST COMPLIMENTS TO CLOSE YOUR SALE

The easy way to find and use honest compliments is to avoid tactless comments such as, "I was just in the neighborhood so I thought I'd drop in and see if you had decided to buy the one hundred widgets we talked about last month. Our special offer is still good."

Let's look a little more closely at this comment, because it is one that is still thoughtlessly used by salesmen from time to time. No busy man is complimented when you tell him that you dropped in on a whim, or just because it happened to be the convenient thing to do. This does violence to his ego and indicates that your call is not really important. Instead, compliment him and appeal to his ego by saying something like this—"I particularly wanted to see you today because our special offer on widgets is still good. Just okay the order for the one hundred you expressed an interest in last month. You can effect a substantial savings and I'll see that the widgets are shipped promptly."

When you want to close a sale on widgets or anything else, make your buyer feel important. This appeals to his ego and closes your sale.

You can always pay your customer an honest compliment as you work on his ego to close your sale. There may be little about him that is pleasing. Yet, there is something you can compliment him on or about. You can compliment him on a clean store, or attractive office, a splendid library, an uncluttered desk, a new pair of shoes, a bright necktie, and on and on. Of course, when you compliment a prospective buyer you are not asking him to do anything. The compliment is a preliminary that pampers his ego and leads to the appeal. Any appeal you use must lead to action in the form of a closed sale. Your compliment must be given in that frame if it is to do much for you or your customer.

Janet Carson sells a bookkeeping service. She called on Sam Kaplan, agent for a moving company. Sam was in the warehouse barking orders and loading furniture. He greeted Janet with, "Well, what do you want?"

"About ten minutes of your time, Mr. Kaplan," Janet answered.

"I'm busy," said Mr. Kaplan.

"Yes," said Janet. "That's why I want to see you. Your friends tell me that you can do more work than anyone they know."

"That's about right," agreed Mr. Kaplan.

"Well," Janet responded, "give me that ten minutes. I want to explain how you can get even more done."

The upshot of this interview that began with a compliment on Mr. Kaplan's work prowess was that Janet sold her bookkeeping service to Sam Kaplan to enable him to "do even more and keep up a hot pace for his men."

Sam Kaplan probably felt that his decision was based on business logic and nothing more. True, Janet's proposal was a service he much needed. However, Janet knows she would never have gotten Mr. Kaplan to stop and listen without that compliment regarding his work habits. She, like any skilled salesperson, used an ego appeal to close her sale. That's one of the reasons Carson Accounting Services continues to grow. Gushing won't close sales, but finding and using honest compliments will, as Janet will attest.

IGNORING THE EGO CAN SHOOT YOU DOWN

Selling might be more simple if all a salesman had to know was his prices, his sales manual, and his merchandise. Today, though, it's a lot more challenging than that. Customers are sophisticated. They demand more than a mechanical performance. In fact, the successful salesman in today's market must have a keen knowledge of human behavior, or psychology if that sounds better, in order to close a big share of sales. Ignoring the ego can shoot you down in this profession.

One sales executive puts it this way: "The businessman salesman of today has to know people. He has to know what makes people tick, what motivates them, what they will respond to; and more, what he can do to get them to do what he knows they should do. He must be able to do this while never for a moment losing sight of the technical aspects of selling. Only a professional can close sales today. On the plus side he is better paid for doing so than ever before."

Off hand, you might think it a bit ridiculous that a salesman had to consider a fertilizer dealer's ego. Delvin Jackson was rudely reminded that every man has an ego, and that every salesman must recognize it if he intends to keep closing sales with any customer. Delvin had a right to feel that he had Lebanon Farm and Supply pretty well tied up and secured. He had routinely closed sales for liquid fertilizer with this customer for six years. You can imagine his shock when Alva Foreman of Lebanon Farm and Supply told him he had signed with a competitor for the coming year. Naturally Delvin asked why, but he really didn't learn why until Alva Foreman's partner laid it on the line one month later. He explained that the young salesman from Delvin's biggest competitor had come in and said, "I want your business. I can offer you as good a deal as anybody, as you know, but that's not why I want to sell you. I need to learn this business and you have the reputation of knowing more about the fertilizer business than anyone else in the area. I would appreciate your business, but I would appreciate the privilege of learning from you even more."

It took Delvin two years to get his business back. He knew he had shot himself out of the saddle by taking too much for granted and ignoring a customer's ego. It's a mistake he hasn't made since.

Remember Delvin's mistake. Stay high in the saddle as you close your sale by appealing to your prospect or customer's ego.

HOW TO BEAT THE COMPETITION
BY USING THE EGO APPEAL TO CLOSE YOUR SALE

We have just had a look at how a young salesman came in the back door and closed a sale that Delvin Jackson thought was all his. You can beat the competition and close your sale with the ego appeal in much the same way. Howard Levinson, a veteran shoe salesman, closed a sale and gained a new account worth $9000 a year to him with this technique.

Howard was well aware that Dyker Shoe Stores enjoyed a healthy business. However, Dyker sold inferior shoes at a low mark-up. All their advertising was keyed to the price theme. Both Dyker stores had the image of a low-end discounter. Despite this, as Howard knew, Carlton Dyker, owner of Dyker Shoe Stores, travelled with the country club set. Howard used this valuable customer background information effectively. Here is how:

Howard got down to business quickly as he always did. "Mr. Dyker," he said, "We have a number of mutual friends. I see you with them at the club. Yet I never see them in your store. Isn't it obvious that you are overlooking a lot of lucrative business when you stick to the cheapest shoes you can buy? Your friends all wear shoes—good shoes such as my line. Not only could a man of your social attainments make money with this line of fine shoes, but in your case your social position would be enhanced even as your profits grew. Here is a suggested order for our new fall styles. You owe it to yourself as well as your friends to get these shoes in as soon as possible. This brochure explains our co-op advertising plan to help you get off to a flying start."

The ego appeal worked. Howard closed his sale and now enjoys a big chunk of business that his competitor formerly had all to himself.

Use the ego appeal to beat your competition fair and square. It will not only boost your own ego, it will also make friends and money for you. Ask Howard about that.

EGO IS NOT THE SAME AS CONCEIT

When you consider the ego appeal as the tool to close a sale keep this in mind: Ego is not the same thing as conceit. Ego is self-esteem, as we noted earlier. Self-conceit is vanity—which is not a closing tool.

When you close your sale with the ego appeal you are dealing with shades of pride, personal satisfaction, self-respect, status, rank, position, and other powerful human emotions. No prospect is totally immune to the intense part emotion plays in the consummation of a satisfying business deal.

Often several appeals are put together in order to close a sale. This is good strategy. When you tie concrete logic to a powerful emotional appeal such as the ego appeal, your closed sale becomes a reality.

HOW TO USE YOUR OWN EGO TO CLOSE MORE SALES

The experienced top-notch salesman knows that his own ego plays a considerable part in the number of sales he closes day in and day out. It is the personal pride that a big money salesman has that gives him the drive to maintain strict self-discipline. It is ego that leads him to study continually in order to be the best informed salesman in his field. There is no such thing as a leader without a bit of ego (you may call it self-confidence, pride, self-esteem).

To illustrate how a salesman's opinion of himself (ego) works, I once heard an inspirational speaker tell of a salesman who made $10,000 a year in a desolate territory. After several years in this wasteland his company decided he had earned a chance to make more money. He was transferred to a productive territory where the salesman in that territory had been making $20,000 a year regularly. But the salesman, now in the $20,000 territory, still managed to make only $10,000 a year. The trouble was that he thought of himself as a $10,000 a year man. He would probably still be making $10,000 a year, but, as the speaker related, a wise sales executive diagnosed his problem. He went to work on the salesman's ego and soon had the man moving up. His closed sales ratio grew right along with his new-found ego, thanks to the intelligent guidance of his superior.

This case is not unlike the salesman who said to his $100,000 a year friend, "Gee, I'd be satisfied with half that much!" Until he gets his ego up to where it should be, he probably will always be satisfied with "half that much."

Buyers, prospects, and customers are prone to take a salesman at his own estimate. Joe Blumenthal, an experienced valve salesman, was well aware of this. He called on a confectionary manufacturer for the first time. He was quickly told by the purchasing agent that the firm's mechanic had been having problems with leaky valves. So far nothing and nobody had solved the problem.

"Do you think you're big enough to whip our problem?" the purchasing agent bluntly asked Joe.

Joe wasn't squeamish. His salesman's ego was in good working order. He answered, "Yes, sir, I have the valves to do the job, and if I can't pinpoint your problem our engineering department can."

"If you can do that the business is yours from now on," said the purchasing agent.

Joe Blumenthal was as good as his word and so was the purchasing agent. Joe found the problem, supplied the valves, and gave the mechanic the assistance he needed. Since this master salesman used his ego to close the original sale, the confectionery manufacturer has tripled his production facilities. Joe is enjoying the increased business right along with his loyal customer.

CONCENTRATE YOUR OWN EGO ON THE CLOSED SALE

Naturally, the strong superior salesman is careful not to flaunt his ego. This would be like a slap in the face to the customer. Flaunting your self-confidence (ego) would only serve to stiffen your prospect's or customer's resistance. Don't wear your ego on your sleeve. Keep it sizzling, but keep it controlled like the mighty force it is. Concentrate it on the closed sale just as Joe Blumenthal did.

PURVES' INSTANT POINTERS ON HOW TO CLOSE
BY APPEALING TO THE PROSPECT'S EGO

- Be sincere and honest as you appeal to the prospect's or customer's ego.
- The tougher they are the more they want their ego pampered.
- Gushing won't close a sale, but finding and using an honest compliment will.
- Ignoring the ego can shoot you down.
- You can use the ego appeal to beat your competition fair and square.
- Ego is not the same as conceit.
- Concentrate your own ego on the closed sale.

18

How to Close When the Prospect Won't Talk

It is an exasperating experience to work with a prospect who won't talk. Strong men have given up in despair and have left the sale for someone else to close. It is not the easiest thing in the world to deal with a man who won't say yes and who won't say no. He is not voiceless, but he has a problem.

Whatever the reason that he cannot or will not talk, that is his problem. The salesman's problem is to close the sale. It is easier to close the sale with the prospect who won't talke when we understand why he won't talk. Here are some of the reasons, real or imaginary, that often plague this prospect. If nothing else they afford him an excuse to hide behind an annoying delaying tactic. The following is, at best, a partial list.

The prospect—

- Is testing the salesman.
- Is seeking to intimidate the salesman.
- Has an inborn mistrust of people.
- Is trying to wring concessions from the salesman.
- Has an inferiority complex.
- Considers this tactic a smart business technique.
- Is trying to embarrass the salesman and throw him off guard.
- Is hiding behind a no-decision shell.
- Is afflicted with a cautious bitterness.
- May have a mind that is encrusted with barnacles.
- Considers his role as the big strong silent man an impressive, commanding posture.
- May not be aware that he is not communicating.
- May be trying to boost his ego by baiting the salesman.
- May be a nice guy despite his uncooperative attitude.

In any case, the point is to close the sale whatever hang-up the prospect who won't talk may have. It is not necessary to thoroughly psychoanalyze the prospect. Experienced salesmen have closed the uncommunicative customer time and again. It is done every day. Let's examine some of the techniques these successful men use to close sales when they confront the no-talk prospect.

DON'T ACCEPT SILENCE AS A TURN-DOWN

The sales interview is not over just because the prospect won't talk readily. When he is not talking, he is not saying, "No." Don't accept silence as a turn-down. Instead, use the following ideas to get your prospect to open up. You can then close your sale.

ASK A QUESTION AND WAIT FOR AN ANSWER

One of the most effective ways to get the stone-faced prospect to talk is to ask him a question. Then sit back and wait for an answer. Look your silent friend in the face and hold his gaze. Don't flinch, squirm, or move. Look expectant and at ease. Wait. Wait as long as necessary. Wait until the clam opens up and answers. You will find that he is human after all. And further, you may find that he really wanted you to close your sale all along. You will never know, though, if you weaken and start talking again before the prospect answers your question.

Mike Halstead works national accounts for the construction and consumer products division of Bowman Specialties Company. He faced Mr. J.B. Schmidt, who sat with arms folded across his chest. For a full ten minutes neither man spoke. Here is what had preceded the ten minute stand-off.

Mike had called on Schmidt, Incorporated, a large hardware distributor who concentrated heavily on the building trades. Mike had a new heavy duty hammer tacker aptly named the Star Fastener. He had demonstrated his new tool to Mr. Schmidt, explaining that the Star Fastener was husky enough to drive heavier, longer staples with wide crowns. This heavy duty tool was ideal for tough jobs requiring extra holding power and penetration, Mike explained. He detailed how the Star Fastener was especially suited for fastening plywood on subflooring, nailing asphalt shingles to roofs, could be used on shipping crates, in applying metal lath, and was ideal for a variety of other industrial and building material applications. He pointed out the construction features of his prize, too, such as, high carbon hardened steel working parts, all-steel construction, jam proof mechanism, retractible striking edge, easy-grip handle, and full strip loading capacity of heavy gauge staples with 1″ crown and ¾″ leg length.

Mr. Schmidt had listened, with folded arms and had said not a word. Finally Mike had asked, "Mr. Schmidt, don't you agree that this is the finest tack hammer you have ever seen?" He had waited for a full ten minutes without moving a muscle. Finally, his prospect showed signs of life. Mr. Schmidt unfolded his arms, picked up the Star Fastener from the desk where Mike had placed it directly in front of him and said, "Yes, I think it must be."

With that the lines of communication and reason were opened. Mike asked for the order and closed his sale. His commission was only two hundred and fifty dollars on the original sale, but the repeat business has been more than gratifying.

If Mike had caved in after asking his question, some other iron-willed salesman would be enjoying all that repeat business today.

Stacy Channan is a spirited young lady who has the responsibility of promoting and selling the Big Lakes Lodge and Resort as a convention center. Her success has been remarkable. Here's how she handled a tough local entrepreneur who wouldn't talk.

Lester Knox, of Knox Enterprises, had a sales force of thirty. Twice a year he had held sales meetings (which the wives also attended) at the same old facility where his father had conducted meetings years before. Stacy went after him to bring his semi-annual meetings to Big Lakes Lodge. It had taken three persistent efforts just to set up the interview. Now Stacy had thoroughly briefed Mr. Knox on all the advantages of Big Lakes Lodge—superior meeting rooms, large comfortable individual rooms for the salesmen and their wives, year-around swimming pool, tennis courts, golf course, and other modern amenities. The food service was superb, too, Stacy enthusiastically explained. As a clincher, the Knox company could hold their meetings at the attractive resort for only 5% more than their old convention center charged. Mr. Knox merely gave her the silent treatment.

"You are proud of your sales force aren't you, Mr. Knox?" Stacy asked. Then she leaned back with an expectant air to wait for an answer. As Stacy puts it, it seemed like an eternity before Mr. Knox finally said, "If I were not I would fire the whole bunch."

"That's pretty emphatic," said Stacy. "So why don't you show them that you're a little proud of them. Nothing would boost their morale and show your appreciation more than going first class with them. Is there any reason in the world why you shouldn't do just that?"

There was another period of rather frosty silence. Stacy held her ground with dignity, and without being the first to break the silence. Then she discovered that Knox could actually smile! He stuck out his hand and said, "Okay, young lady, if you will help us by setting up the whole thing for us."

Stacy promptly agreed that was exactly what she had in mind. The deal was closed.

Stacy has sold bigger conventions. She still says that this one was her most profitable, because she learned a fundamental technique in how to handle a prospect who won't talk.

HOW TO MAINTAIN A STRONG ATTITUDE WHEN THE PROSPECT WON'T TALK

One of the hallmarks of the superior salesman is his ability to maintain a strong, positive attitude under trying conditions. It is an absolute that you show a strong attitude when the prospect won't talk. One sign of wavering and old iron-jaw may never open his mouth, even to say good-bye.

Here's a basic thought to help you keep a strong attitude when the prospect won't talk. Never consider this prospect, or any other customer or prospect, a problem. He is not the problem. The only problem you have in this situation is to close the sale. Focus on the closing. Direct your energies to that end and your attitude will stay strong until the job is finished.

Walter Hudsmith sells a line of mixers, agitators, and blenders to chemical, food, and fertilizer manufacturers. When he had called twice and had been given the cold, silent treatment by a prospective customer, he began to feel that he had a problem instead of a prospect. Walter knew his product and he knew his own abilities. He also knew what to do when he felt his attitude sagging. He followed the rule many outstanding salesmen use when they are backed into a corner. He sat down and put it all on paper. Here is what Walter calls his attitude chart. He makes such a chart for any difficult case. Walter reports that these charts have helped him close a lot of tough sales where big money has been involved. Here is the chart that Walter used to keep on track and close a sale when his prospect wouldn't talk. It earned Walter a $2500 commission and a new account.

WALTER HUDSMITH'S ATTITUDE CHECK CHART

Negative Thoughts	Sales Closing Attitude
• This prospect is unfriendly	• He needs my help.
• This prospect is a sourpuss.	• This man may be unsure of himself.
• This guy won't talk!	• I can do something to get this prospect to respond.
• I'll bypass this sphinx.	• I'll close this sale and move on to the next one.
• I don't have to call on anybody so rude.	• Somebody is going to close this sale. I'm that man.
• I'll tell the big dummy off.	• I'll treat this prospect with genuine respect just as I do all my customers.
• This prospect is bullying me.	• I'm a pro. I won't be side-tracked by somebody else's negative attitude.
• I will outsmart this joker.	• I will give this man sound reasons to buy from me.
• He doesn't deserve a good deal.	• I am going to make this prospect glad that he bought from me.
• He doesn't like me.	• There is nothing personal in his attitude. I don't have to kiss him. My job is to close the sale.

As every experienced salesman recognizes, a strong positive attitude is mandatory when a sale is at stake. It is never more so than when the salesman is dealing with a prospect who won't talk.

Profit by Walter Hudsmith's idea. Make your own personal attitude chart. List every negative thought that has crept into your mind. Offset each of these sales-killers with a strong statement from your positive attitude. Seeing your strong attitude on paper will push any defeating ideas into the background. Then you can get back to business and close your sale just as Walter Hudsmith did.

MAKE THE PROSPECT DO <u>SOMETHING</u>

It is hard for a man to be involved in anything and still say nothing. When your prospect won't talk give him something to do; get him involved. Hand him something. Here are a few ideas.

HAVE HIM DO SOME ARITHMETIC FOR YOU

If your presentation involves figures, hand pen and pencil to your silent friend and ask him to do some arithmetic for you.

John Craig has a line of cosmetics. His is a little known, small manufacturer covering a limited territory. Naturally, there are plans for expansion. John, as head of marketing, figures heavily in the future plans of his company. And for good reasons—he closes sales.

Recently John was interviewing the buyer for a big supermarket. This supermarket featured a complete drug department with everything from cosmetics to prescription service. John went into his thoroughly professional presentation. The buyer sat attentively, but with his lips tightly compressed. One thing John already knew was that his product offered a 20% higher mark-up than did the competing product. John handed his prospect his pencil and notebook. "Here," he said, "write down the amount of sales that you enjoyed last year on your current brand."

When the prospect had jotted down this figure John said, "Now deduct your cost to get your gross profit."

Next John said, "OK, add 20% to that profit figure and you will be close to how much more you could make on my line. How much would that amount to?"

"Well," Harvey Wayne, the buyer, eventually said, "it would come to about $3000 extra."

"Don't you owe it to your firm to consider the extra money that your figures show could be made by adding my line of cosmetics?"

Harvey Wayne doodled awhile then said, "These figures are hard to dispute. Let's see what kind of opening order we can put together."

Have your customer who won't talk do some arithmetic for you. Anything that gets him involved in your presentation can add to your income just as it did to John Craig's in this instance.

One institutional food salesman, Reid Kuhn, specializes in selling concentrated breakfast beverages to volume users. Recently he encountered a purchasing agent who wouldn't talk. His prospect was not only a dietitian, but the buyer for the food service department of the concern. This lady had a lot of mileage on her and wasn't eager to do anything new. The breakfast business in this chain of restaurants was tremendous and our salesman friend meant to close his sale and get his share of that business. Here's how he broke the ice and moved the prospect to speak.

First, he placed a 32 ounce tin of orange juice concentrate in front of the prospect. Then he handed her his pen and a piece of note paper.

"Will you do something for me?" he asked. "You don't have to say a word if you don't want to. First, write down $3.50, which is your cost on one can of this concentrate. O.K., now put down 32 ounces and multiply that by six. What do you get?"

"I get 192 ounces, of course," his prospect replied.

"Now," the salesman instructed, "divide that by 8 ounces, the size of your larger serving of orange juice."

"I get 24, what else?" said the lady.

"So far so good," said the salesman. "Now multiply that by 60 cents and tell me what you get."

"The answer is $14.40," affirmed the prospect.

"Right," said John. "Now deduct $3.50 and give me the result."

"Ten dollars and ninety cents," was the reply.

"That is your profit on only one tin of the concentrate base, since you add five tins of water to make the finished juice drink. Don't you agree that the quality of our product and the profit your company will realize from it, along with the convenience of serving the product, justifies an order today?"

The lady of few words said, "Yes, but not today. We have enough on hand for two weeks. Wait until then and deliver fifty cases to our distribution warehouse. I'll prepare the requisition for you now."

Reid said his commissions from the restaurant chain now goes a long way toward paying his substantial income tax every year. Getting the no-talk prospect to do some arithmetic can close your sale and make things a bit easier for an aggressive money-making salesman.

THERE IS MORE THAN ONE GOOD GIMMICK TO GET THE NO-TALK PROSPECT INTO THE ACT

A good gimmick is not a trick, it is a sales technique or feature that is not immediately apparent to the prospect. It is a good device to use to get the no-talk prospect involved so that he will open up and take action. Here are a few of these features, or techniques, that are tested devices which can close sales with the no-talk prospect or customer. Use your own experience and sales expertise to find appropriate gimmicks to close your sale. There's more than one good gimmick to get the no-talk prospect or customer into the act. The following will give you ideas on which to build.

- If you are demonstrating a machine or something with movable parts, put it in your silent prospect's hands. Invite him to try it. Show him how to make it work. Politely insist that he see for himself what a marvelous invention it is. Get excited and let your excitement rub off on him. Ask him if it isn't the best on the market just as you have said. Ask him if it doesn't meet every criterion that his particular need dictates. Enthuse about your product's exclusive or unique features. When you ask him a question remember to wait for an answer. When he answers ask for the order. Keep your whole performance focused on the closing.

- Whatever you are selling you can give the silent type something to look at, something to examine. If it is tangible, place it in his hands and go on as in the preceding paragraph. If it is intangible, you can show him your proposal in black and white. If he volunteers no reaction use the "ask a question and wait" technique. Force him to talk as you involve him. That is the only way he can say yes when you are ready to close.

- Get your tight-mouthed prospect to involve every sense you can in order to arouse his interest and enthusiasm to the point where he will talk. If he can feel your product, see that he does. If he can hear it, make sure that he listens. If he can smell it, give him a good whiff. If he can taste it, give him a taste. If he can see it, be sure that he sees all of it.

It cannot be emphasized too often that as you lead your no-talk prospect into active involvement in your presentation, you must not be the only one to talk. It this happens you do not have a viable sales presentation; you have a no-win monologue. Ask that pertinent question and wait for the answer. The more answers you get the closer you get to closing your sale—which is the whole point as you work with Mr. Lockjaw.

PURVES' INSTANT POINTERS ON HOW TO CLOSE
WHEN THE PROSPECT WON'T TALK

- The point is to close the sale whatever the hang-up the prospect may have.
- Don't accept silence as a turn-down.
- Ask a question and *wait* for an answer.
- Keep a strong, positive attitude when the prospect won't talk.
- The prospect or customer is not the problem. The problem is to close the sale.
- Make the prospect do something.
- Have the prospect do some arithmetic for you.
- There is more than one good gimmick to get the no-talk prospect into the act.
- Closing the sale is the whole point as you work with Mr. Lockjaw.

19

How to Close with Word Pictures

A healthy, adequate, working vocabulary is a requisite in any field of endeavor. No matter the other attributes a man has, if his vocabulary is weak he has great difficulty attaining his goals or reaching his potential. The reason is obvious. It takes a strong vocabulary to explain a majestic idea in simple and understandable terms. Without proper communication (which demands a responsible vocabulary) ideas, no matter how brilliantly conceived, cannot be shared. In the same sense, a worthy cause will perish unless it is supported by an intelligent and appealing vocabulary. To bring the point directly home, a weak vocabulary cannot create desire or motivate people to action. A skimpy, starved, ragged vocabulary does not close sales—it kills them.

This does not mean that the salesman is expected to speak with the precision and exactness of a senior lecturer in English at a major university. Nor does it mean that he should employ flowery speech and big words. It does mean that the salesman must appreciate that the words which comprise his vocabulary are his chief working tools. It does mean that he has a responsibility to keep these tools razor-sharp and in working order. Your vocabulary, the inflection in your voice, plus your professional speech habits, make up your most priceless sales kit. Nobody can take it from you. It is yours alone to use wisely. When you do, you will close sales with more ease than you thought possible.

HOW TO KEEP YOUR SALES-CLOSING VOCABULARY ALIVE AND UP-TO-DATE

The closed sale starts with an idea. You plan to explain, describe, picture, and define something in such a way that your prospect or customer will buy it without delay. Every word you use must be a word that moves your presentation closer to the closed sale. Since you are a professional, your vocabulary must have a professional flavor. It is imperative that you not only use good grammar, but that your professional and technical language be current and correct. The man selling locomotive components will use much terminology that would be useless, if not foreign, to the life insurance salesman intent on closing a case. Whatever your product, your vocabulary must reflect the fact that you are well-versed and up-to-date in your field. Here are suggestions from sales leaders in their respective fields. Each suggestion is based on long experience and illustrates how these businessmen keep their sales-closing vocabulary up-to-the-minute.

- Read everything pertaining to your field that you can lay your hands on.
- Subscribe to periodicals and trade journals that cover the latest advances in product knowledge and marketing techniques in your profession or business.
- Attend seminars regularly.
- Cultivate the acquaintance of the leaders in your sphere of activity.
- Read books by authorities on the marketing, selling, and production of your product or products.
- Set aside regular study time to keep abreast of what is new in your field.
- Analyze and determine the meaning and application of any new words you discover while studying your product, or while studying new techniques to be used in selling your product.
- To enrich your vocabulary, and to round out your knowledge, read on a variety of subjects.
- Take review courses in grammar and speech. These may be evening classes or short courses.
- Build a personal vocabulary of strong closing words and statements that you can utilize when needed to close a sale.

There is no magic formula to guarantee that you will close every sale quickly and easily under any and all circumstances. There is word magic though. Word magic will make you more professional and will speed the closing of your sale. Use the above suggestions to build your own word magic vocabulary. Use it as other professionals use it—to close sales and make money.

I had a friend in St. Louis, Missouri, a few years ago who was never content until he had his first million dollars in life insurance sales each year. After the first million he just kept going. I heard him explain the secret of his success. He said, "I read everything written on the subject of life insurance and the selling of life insurance. I mean to know every word in the business and I want to know exactly how to use it to close sales."

His idea of building and using the word magic in his business is sound. He no longer lives in St. Louis. He lives in New York and has a plush office in one of those towering new skyscrapers. He also has the word "Vice President" immediately below his name on the door of that office.

Your sales-closing vocabulary is your word magic key to success—as every proponent of bigger and better selling has demonstrated again and again. Follow their example and keep yours alive and fire-balling. It is the most personal sales-closing tool you will ever possess.

WORDS ARE TOOLS THAT CLOSE SALES

Words are tools that close sales. Let us hammer this into our minds. Words are to the salesman what the brush and canvas are to the artist. Words paint pictures that create desire and call for action. Words inspire, move, zoom, dive, guide, threaten, cajole, promise, and deliver. Words erase confusion, remove doubt, and lead to conviction. The skilled salesman respects the awesome power of a finely honed vocabulary. He uses it to paint word pictures that close sale after sale.

Recently I walked into a shoe store in the biggest shopping mall in our town. Two pairs of shoes had caught my eye. One pair was ten dollars more than the other, though they looked alike to me. I asked the young man twiddling his thumbs nearby what the difference was in the shoes. He came over and looked at both pairs of shoes then said numbly, "Ten dollars, hee-hee, I guess."

Well, hee-hee, I walked out with my money still in my pocket and went to a bustling shop at the other end of the mall. A young fellow acknowledged my presence at once and said he would be with me as soon as he finished with the customer he was then helping. I found the identical shoes similarly priced. I asked this young man the same question. He painted a picture of the difference for me with words that were simple, direct, and clear-cut. Pointing to the more expensive pair he began:

"This pair has leather uppers and leather soles. The other is made of man-made materials. The leather provides for ventilation while still keeping your feet dry and comfortable. This pair has a steel shank support and a non-slip leather heel-grip piece. It is double cushioned inside for extra comfort. True, the shoes cost ten dollars more, but as you can see, the extra features make it worth more. It is the latest style and has proven to be popular with our regular customers. It comes in two colors, tan and black. Here, try on a pair."

I tried on a pair. I bought two pairs—one tan, one black.

The shoes I bought were identical to the shoes I saw in the first store. The reason I bought at the second store was, of course, because the second salesman had command of his sales-closing words. He knew how to use his tools. As a result, he got what he wanted and I got what I wanted. This is the ideal closed sale.

Life insurance salesmen rely strongly on word pictures to close sales. The application blank alone never closes life insurance sales. Words are the tools that do the job.

Life insurance salesmen paint pictures of security, comfort, happiness, and peace of mind. They talk of the money that will provide a home and education for the children should the father die prematurely. They picture the desolation and heartbreak of a widow losing her home and being forced out into the labor market because a husband failed to act in time. Then they glowingly describe the assurance that the wife can remain in their happy home, debt free and with adequate funds to stay home and properly raise the children in a loving atmosphere. The husband can guarantee all this with insurance as soon as he signs the application. Too, they address businessmen with the same dynamic, life-like, motivating words as they close sales time and again on key man and partnership cases.

Words are not the exclusive domain of any one industry. They are the chief closing tool of any salesman selling any product.

Jack Huckabee operates a saw mill. He specializes in creosote-treated fence posts which he sells to farmers and cattlemen. He paints word pictures to sell his fence posts. He uses strong words such as rot-resistant, easy-to-use, and long-lasting. He describes the ease of setting the posts and attaching any kind of fencing desired. He dwells on the utility and economy of his product. He paints pictures of the safety, security, and convenience his posts make possible. He visualizes with words the well-ordered and efficient operation his posts will make possible for his farmer and cattlemen friends. And he does it with terms that are familiar to his clientele.

Jack can tell you that words are tools that close sales. In the five years he has been in business his volume has climbed an average of 20% each year.

AVOID FUZZY WORDS THAT DEMAND NOTHING

As you already know, Chapter 13 in this book also deals with the salesman's working vocabulary. The words you use to close sales are important enough to deserve extra attention. However, it is just as important to weed out weak words as it is to cultivate good strong words. It is deceptively easy to slip into a faulty speech habit. Dull, lifeless cliches have a way of slithering into our speech. Here are some ideas to keep from being trapped by these nasty little sales-killers.

Fuzzy words, such as fabulous, sensational, terrific, wow, are words that add nothing to the sales presentation. They demand no action, and for that reason do nothing to move the sale to a logical closing. Here is how Jesse Sovich, an investments salesman, culled useless words from his sales presentation.

Jesse has two college degrees. He also possesses an abundance of native intelligence. So when he slipped into a sales slump last year he decided to analyze his sales presentation. He set about it in a no-holds-barred fashion. He took a cassette with him on his next three calls. With the prospect's permission he recorded every word of his presentation. That night he sat with a note pad and pen in his hand and played the tapes back to himself. What he heard was surprising and revealing. He quickly learned why he was in a slump, and why he had failed to close any of the three prospects that day.

Jesse was appalled at the number of times he heard himself say "You know." He was using this pointless utterance thoughtlessly; indeed, without realizing that he was punctuating his speech with such an inane expression. He also was dismayed to hear himself say "I" three times as often as he said "you." He noted, too, that his voice lacked the warmth and inflection that he had believed he was injecting into every presentation.

After listening to all three tapes and making notes as he did so, Jesse did two things. First, he made a list of powerful selling words that fit into his product category. His list included such words as growth, extra income, retirement funds, security, benefits, protection from inflation, dividends, earnings, leaders, sound companies, now, for instance, examples, economy, performance, history, and *you, you, you*.

With this list of working words before him, Jesse restructured his presentation. He squeezed out every fuzzy word and eliminated meaningless phrases and expressions. From beginning to end his presentation was aimed at the closed sale. His presentation was beefed up with the urgency and logic of closing now.

When Jesse Sovich kicked out the fuzzy words that demanded nothing, his new presentation developed enough muscle to triple his closed sales in one month. Since Jesse works on straight commission, it follows that this smart strategy also tripled his income in thirty days.

Fuzzy words that demand nothing are expensive. Kick them out as Jesse Sovich did. The closed sales resulting from your vibrant, compelling word pictures can be spectacular.

HOW TO FIND POWER WORDS TO CLOSE YOUR SALE

There can be no prescriptive list of words that will close each and every sale under any and all circumstances. Salesmen, prospects, and customers do their thinking in words. Each are individuals. You, the salesman, must be an observant, analytical thinker. Whenever possible you should analyze your prospect or customer ahead of time. If not, you must quickly analyze the situation on the spot. The purpose of such an objective analysis is to determine the strongest possible appeal to close your sale. When this is done, you can find the most effective power words to close your sale at once.

Here are some examples to spark your imagination and enable you to instantly select power words that will close your sale.

When your prospect or customer's primary concern is profit—use power words such as these:

Repeat business	**Customer appeal**
Profit margin	**Co-op advertising**
Fast turnover	**Promotional**
Money	**Inventory control**
Cash Flow	**Guarantee**
Dependable source	**Fast delivery**

When your prospect, or customer's primary concern is security—use such words as:

Safe	Proven
Tested	Guaranteed
Stable	Established
Researched	Warranty
Service	Honesty
Tried	Reputation
True	Character

When your prospect or customer's main interest is status—use words such as these:

Prestige	Pride
Esteem	Joy
You	Peers
Position	Achievement
Respect	Envy
Success	Leader
Rank	Stature
Quality	Proud
Delight	High

You can find such power words to close your sale whether your prospect's keenest interest is health, love, cleanliness, education, or any of the myriad obsessions or desires that every prospect or customer has. The key to the quick closed sale is to use your experience and the salesman's sharp intellect to spot the strongest appeal to use on the customer you are facing at the moment. You may discover several appeals. Take advantage of every one. Marshal your power words that suit the occasion. Then you are ready to close your sale and collect your pay.

Alan Weeks, an expert salesman who sells encyclopedias and educational materials to schools and other institutions, has a program to build a vocabulary of power words that close sales. I highly recommend it to you.

Alan always has a dictionary with him wherever his travels take him. He uses his dictionary to learn the meaning of unfamiliar words. If it is a power word he repeats it over and over until it is fixed in his mind. Then he uses it aloud in several sentences. Further, when he does not discover at least one new word as he works each day, he goes to his dictionary that night and selects a new power word. He follows the same routine of repeating that word until it is glued in his mind. He uses it not merely to build a more impressive vocabulary—his objective is to uncover more sales closing tools.

It's amazing the way this simple idea works. As Alan Weeks points out, one new power word a day adds up to three hundred and sixty-five new closing tools in one year. In two years the figure becomes seven hundred and thirty. This arsenal of closing tools actually represents a bigger vocabulary than the whole vocabulary some people use!

Don't hesitate to put Alan's idea to work. He is his firm's top money maker. He credits his success to the power words he finds and uses to close sale after sale. Power words paint powerful pictures that can close your sale fast.

HOW TO USE ENOUGH WORDS
TO GET THE JOB DONE AND NO MORE

As you paint word pictures to close your sale you are not trying to indulge your artistic talents for the sheer fun of it. You are pursuing a business project. Don't blow up your canvas. Use only enough words to get the job done and no more. Here's how:

- Keep control of the sales interview. Don't waste time and words by being led into discussions that have nothing to do with the closed sale. If your prospect goes off on a tangent, politely but firmly lead him back to the business at hand. Restrict your words to the business at hand. Put your power words to work to capture and hold your prospect or customer's attention. Close at the first signal. You will be ahead and so will your customer.

- Refrain from socializing on your sales call. Most successful salesmen just naturally have a great number of personal friends among their customers. This is a healthy sign. But it is not a healthy thing to socialize on a sales call. If this happens, a mess of banal conversation can take place. Words will fly right and left without getting near the closed sale. Confine your words to the urgent business at hand. Paint a business picture with your power words. This is the direct way to your closed sale.

- Avoid firetrap topics that can become word-filled conflagrations. Do not be drawn into any discussion of religion or politics during a sales presentation. People have short fuses where these subjects are concerned. One wrong word and the only picture you will paint will be one of disaster. As a matter of fact, it is likely to be a gloomy affair if the presentation strays for any reason. Keep on target. Use your power words to get what you came after—the closed sale.

Fuzzy and superfluous words are sales-killers. Use only enough words to get the job done and no more. Do as the experts do—use your power words to paint a sales-closing picture, then get out as soon as the job is done. More than one sale has been lost during idle chitchat after the sale had been closed. Stick to business on each call. When your business is finished move on to the next sale. This way your word pictures are never wasted. They get the job done for you. The closed sale belongs to you. Wrap it up with race-horse words.

PURVES' INSTANT POINTERS ON HOW TO CLOSE WITH WORD PICTURES

- A healthy working vocabulary is a requisite.
- A ragged vocabulary does not close sales.
- Your vocabulary is your most personal sales kit. Keep it alive and throbbing.
- Words are tools that close sales.
- Words paint pictures that create desire and lead to action.
- Avoid fuzzy words that demand nothing.
- Find and use power words to close your sale.
- Use enough words to get the job done and no more.
- Use race-horse words.

20

Techniques to Use to Close the Sale Under Intimidation Tactics

A customer is the most important person in the world. He can also be mean, insulting, unreasonable, antagonistic, or downright hostile. But these are not the reasons that you call on him. The reason that you call on him is to close your sale. The benefits are the same when you close no matter what the personality of the customer may be. When you work under intimidation tactics follow Benjamin Franklin's admonition: "Write injuries in dust, write benefits in marble." And in this case the benefits referred to are all yours as you close the tough sale.

TECHNIQUE #1:
DON'T BUILD ARTIFICIAL BARRIERS

Fortunately, most people the salesman calls on are friendly and reasonable. Yet, there are still individuals who, for reasons that are hard to explain, feel a great need to be belligerent. They use intimidation tactics on every salesman who walks through the door. When this happens to you, don't build artificial barriers that will stand in the way of your closed sale.

You build an artificial barrier, first of all, if you permit the abusive buyer to make you feel inadequate. Keep in mind that the man who goes off the deep end and tries to browbeat you is the man with a problem. His personality affliction is not your problem. Your only problem is to close the sale. Somebody is going to sell him and make a friend of the poor misguided soul. Make this your objective and do not get into a witless verbal joust with the prospect. You don't get paid for winning arguments. You get paid for closing sales. You can't close the sale if you begin to feel that the buyer is a monster who is too much for you.

Another way to erect an artificial barrier to your closed sale is to become defensive. If you adopt this posture, the bully will have the upper hand. As soon as he senses that he has put you on the defensive he will become more and more intimidating. When this happens, out the door flies your closed sale.

Instead of becoming defensive, look at it this way: You have no reason to squirm or to be apologetic. You are there because you have a legitimate business proposition to present. Your proposition contains far more benefits for Mr. Confused than it does for you. You have benefits to offer that can close your sale. The only way that you can hope to explain the benefits your product or proposition represents is to grab and hold control of the interview. You can do this by turning the tables on the intimidating buyer to put him on the defensive. One effective way to do this is to listen to the threatening prospect until he runs out of steam, and then say something that will yank him back to the business at hand. Here's how one strong salesman did it.

Steve Quinn sells oils and lubricants. He was making his first call on Bert Gullett, maintenance supervisor and a buyer for Red Giant Construction Company. Bert acknowledged Steve's introduction to the effect that the last thing he needed was another grease and oil man perstering him. More, he said, he was too blankety-blank busy to talk to any jerk with something to sell, that salesmen were a pain in his neck anyway, and why didn't Steve hop in his little red wagon and get the heck out of the way—and on and on.

Steve listened and waited. Soon Bert Gullett paused for breath and Steve said matter of factly, "Mr. Gullett, I came here to show you how I can save you some money and give you the finest products on the market. Now that you've got that baloney out of your system, let's get down to business."

Bert Gullett looked a bit dumfounded for a minute. Then he thrust out his hand and said, "Well, if what you have is all that good let's see what it is."

Within ten minutes Steve had closed his sale and had the first of many orders from Red Giant. His first year's commission on the new account amounted to over $2500, which is pretty good pay for ten minutes work. You will note that ten minutes is all the time it took Steve to close his sale when he forcefully brought his intimidating buyer back to the business at hand.

Modify and adapt Steve's technique to your requirements next time you run into an intimidating buyer. Eliminate any artificial barriers and you can close your sale just as Steve did.

TECHNIQUE #2:
SHOW YOUR MUSCLE BUT KEEP YOUR DIGNITY

As an experienced, knowledgeable salesman you will never allow an interview with an intimidating prospect or customer to become a meaningless test of wills. When your buyer is unreasonable in his attitude toward you, of course you must stand your ground and hold fast to your plan to close your sale. Show your muscle, yes, but do not abandon your dignity. One bellicose party at a sales interview is more than enough.

Kenny Hartman, a detail man calling on the medical profession, called on an overworked and irritable physician one Tuesday afternoon. (We will call the physician Dr. Martin Staub to avoid stirring up another hornet's nest.) Kenny had to cool his heels awhile. Finally, after the doctor's secretary reminded him for the third time that Kenny was waiting, Dr. Staub motioned Kenny into his office. He then let loose with a diatribe that would put the proverbial fishwife to shame. Couldn't Kenny see that he was busy? Didn't he have any respect for another man's time? Couldn't he see those patients waiting? All this, mind you, despite the fact that Kenny had been waiting about an hour to keep an appointment the doctor had agreed to the week before.

The first time the doctor paused Kenny quietly said, "Doctor, I've always heard that you were the hardest and meanest man in your profession to call on. I find this difficult to believe. You look far too intelligent to chronically suffer such a poverty of heart. Won't you sit down for a few minutes so that I can bring you up-to-date on our line? You will want to prescribe these products. They will be a great boon to you and to your patients."

The doctor did listen. And he did apologize. He promised Kenny he would give his products every consideration.

Two years later Kenny could say that the doctor was a loyal customer and a good friend. The following year Kenny became a regional supervisor for his firm.

Using forceful closing techniques with honor is a winning proposition. Show your muscle and close your sale when your prospect resorts to intimidation tactics. Do it with dignity. Otherwise you will find yourself working in a disaster area.

TECHNIQUE #3: GIVE THE MAN WHAT HE WANTS
WITHOUT KNUCKLING UNDER

Nobody respects Mr. Milk Toast. Everybody respects and likes the man who can stand up under pressure and do his job. Nowhere is this more evident than in the market place. The intimidating buyer will make life miserable for a weak and hesitant salesman. Conversely, the prospect or customer who habitually relies on intimidating tactics will respect and like the salesman who can give him what he wants without knuckling under. Nobody buys from a salesman who is confused, quaking with fear, and looking for a place to hide.

Justin Rettig sells supplies to mobile home and recreational vehicle manufacturers. Justin earns in excess of $150,000 annually, but he recalls how he was nearly shot out of the saddle in his first year on the road. One of his best prospects was Alfred Francois, president of a concern that manufactured mobile homes and recreation vehicles. Justin says he was badly intimidated on his first two calls. He was ready to throw in the towel until a more experienced and older friend reminded him that Alfred Francois would still be in business even if Justin turned tail and ran. The thought rankled Justin and stiffened his backbone. Back he went for the third time.

He says that an air of intimidation hung like smoke in a closed room as he greeted Mr. Francois once more. This time Justin jumped in with both feet. "Mr. Francois," he started, "I'm here to help you meet your obligation as president of this company."

"What's this all about now?" asked Alfred Francois, rising from his chair.

"Sit down and let's talk about it," was Justin's reply. "You have an obligation to buy at favorable prices and an obligation to get good quality for your money. I can help you do just that. Together we can effect some real economies for your company and continue to maintain your usual high standards. Let's forget my first two visits and get down to business, OK?"

Well, it was OK when Justin stopped knuckling under and gave the man what he wanted all along. Justin earned his first $1000 commission as he closed his sale that day. He says this was the sale and the lesson that started him on the way to his present magnificent income.

When you give the intimidating man what he wants without knuckling under, you can close your sale. The rewards are impressive, as you can see.

TECHNIQUE #4: BE A SECURITY BLANKET FOR THE BELLIGERENT BUYER

Despite all the bluster and thunder of the intimidating buyer, the overwhelming odds are that he is racked by feelings of insecurity and self-doubts. He may subconsciously be afraid that he is likely to make a ghastly buying mistake. To hide his true feelings he creates a facade of tough belligerency. When the salesman can get behind this unhealthy defensive shield, he can reassure the intimidating buyer. The way to do this is to show as politely and firmly as possible that he will profit by doing business with you. You can be a real security blanket for the intimidating prospect or customer once he understands that you are really on his side. This is not always the easiest thing in the world to do, but it is done every day. No matter the personality of the buyer, if he is to be a buyer he must buy. Every time he buys, some determined salesman closes a sale.

Here are a few field-tested ideas to convince the belligerent buyer that you are on his side and sincerely have his interest at heart.

- Show respect for his vociferous ideas. If he were totally incompetent, you wouldn't be calling on him.
- Keep your voice friendly. The tone of your voice conveys your attitude more plainly than your words.
- Keep calm and let him blow off a little steam. When he suddenly realizes that he is the only one making disagreeable noises, he will slow down. That is the time for you to begin, or resume, your presentation. There are examples in this chapter to give you the idea.
- Exude self-confidence. Nothing helps bring the nervous, belligerent buyer into a stable emotional state more than the sight of a self-assured, confident, dominant salesman.
- Always be prepared for the unexpected on any sales call. If you are taken by surprise you may lose your sale before the show begins.
- Be a professional businessman. This is another way to erase the intimidating buyer's doubts. Keep your presentation on a high plateau when under pressure.

- After the sale is closed, assure the belligerent buyer that he has made a smart move. He will feel even more secure when you tell him how you plan to see that he gets everything he expects plus your personal service.

You don't have to baby a belligerent buyer in order to be his security blanket. Accord him every reasonable courtesy. Make the same mature presentation that you do every time you go out to close a sale. The big difference is that this sale may carry some extra satisfaction for you. It is especially gratifying to the most experienced salesman when he closes a worthwhile sale under extraordinary conditions.

One more point: The most destructive personality problems are often those that the afflicted party never recognizes. The habitually intimidating buyer may not realize that he is offensive and unreasonable. Your behavior as an aggressive, dignified salesman may open his eyes a bit. But don't worry overmuch about this. You are not there to remake him. You are there to close your sale on equitable terms.

HOW TO GET THE TOUGH GUY ON YOUR SIDE

When you are obliged to close your sale under intimidation tactics, it may be hard to convince yourself that the tough guy would like to be on your side. It's true though. Any buyer with sense enough to sign an order needs and wants to have an intelligent, tough, understanding salesman as a friend. He may not be able to put this into words, or acknowledge it to himself, but that doesn't alter the fact that he needs and wants you. You will close your sale with the tough guy a lot faster if you accept and act upon this sound psychological thesis.

To get the tough guy on your side (where he wants to be) you will have to be the one to initiate the steps to bring him home. Here are some good, workable techniques to do the job.

- Compliment him warmly. No flattery. Just a sincere little compliment. You can make a few quick observations while he is spouting off and find something complimentary to say when he pauses for breath.

Sam Gattenmeier, a salesman for a canoe and camping equipment distributor, encountered Gus Wicker, a marine dealer, at a major boat show. He approached Mr. Wicker, who had come into his space. Wicker blurted, "Don't try to sell me a bleep-bleep thing. I just came in to see what kind of junk you're peddling. There's not much difference in any of them. They have too many of these shows anyway. Just let me look and I'll be gone."

Sam was not rattled nor overly impressed. He replied, "Mr. Wicker, I can see that you are a busy man with a mind of his own. I appreciate that you don't want to waste any time. I will quickly point out two or three sales features on these canoes, because I know that you want to move your merchandise fast. Note that the screws in our canoes are countersunk. They won't shear off when the canoe scrapes a rocky bottom. This motor mount is available—during this show only—at no cost with each canoe. We can supply electric or gasoline motors. We deliver on our own trucks, have a service department, and carry our own paper. Obviously, you are a smart, no-nonsense operator with profit on his mind. Tell me how many and what size canoes you want and I will see that your order is processed just as you wish. I'm sure we will have no credit problems with a man of your stature, so pick out anything you want. You can save both time and money right now."

Mr. Wicker didn't wilt and become sugary sweet at Sam's words. But Sam had said enough to move Gus Wicker over to his side. He closed his sale, earned a $1350 commission on the first order, and added Mr. Wicker to his list of loyal, profitable accounts.

- Speak the tough guy's language. He respects direct, powerful talk. Don't be offensive. Hang in on the tough guy's level, but on your terms, until your sale is closed. Be positive and politely firm as Sam Gattenmeier did when he met Mr. Wicker. This is an excellent technique to get the tough guy on your side in order to close your sale promptly.

- When you deal with the tough guy, watch your attitude. Don't try to fight back. If you slap him down there is no way that you can close your sale. Your attitude will remain firm and positive when you keep in mind that the closed sale is what you are after. The closed sale, after all, is your badge of victory.

- Don't decide ahead of time that you may not close your sale with Mr. Tough Guy. At least give him a chance to say "Yes." If you weaken and think that you really don't know whether you can close your sale with the tough guy it amounts to this: You are really saying, "I don't want to sell him because he's a little tough talking."

- Keep your thoughts on the closed sale. That will leave no room for negative thinking. Positive thinking and direct action will get the tough guy on your side and open the way to your closed sale.

- Don't be shattered by unreasonable demands that the tough guy may make. He knows right from wrong. If you cave in and grant impossible concessions you are in trouble with the tough guy forevermore. He will ride you to death.

Harry Welek had a tough guy who boldly demanded a TV set in exchange for a big opening order. All Harry had to do to get the tough guy on his side was say, "What do you think would happen to each of us if your boss found out about that?"

It was a sobering thought. Harry had given this buyer sound reasons to buy from him. When he brought the tough guy back to earth, he hit the hot button again and soon had his closed sale.

The tough guy isn't your enemy, he is your prospect. When you have a prospect, the only logical thing to do is close your sale. Use these techniques, plus some of your own, to get the tough guy on your side. Then ask for the order expectantly and matter-of-factly. Close your sale and go on to the next money-making challenge.

LET HIM THINK THE CLOSING IS HIS IDEA

When you close a sale under intimidation tactics, let the buyer think the closing is his idea. If the tough, blustery man feels that he has been out-smarted he isn't likely to be eager to see you again. When he does he will be trying to get even with you instead of sticking to sound business principles.

Any way you look at it, this type is due some credit. There has never been a closed sale until somebody decided to buy something. Sure, most sales are closed because the salesman is aggressive, sharp, and determined to do what he knows is best for him and for his customer. Still, the buyer is due his share of the credit. He was intelligent enough to see the merit in the salesman's proposition, so he bought.

The best way to convey the impression that the closing was the prospect's idea when he has employed intimidating tactics is this: Thank him for the order. Compliment him on his wise decision. Tell him you look forward to many profitable deals with him. Then take your closed sale and get out before the house catches on fire again.

PURVES' INSTANT POINTERS ON TECHNIQUES
TO USE TO CLOSE THE SALE
UNDER INTIMIDATION TACTICS

- Don't build artificial barriers to your closed sale when working under intimidation tactics.
- You have no reason to be defensive or apologetic.
- Show your muscle, but keep your dignity.
- Use forceful closing techniques with honor to avoid working in a disaster area.
- Be a security blanket for the belligerent buyer and close your sale.
- You don't have to baby the belligerent buyer.
- You can get the tough guy on your side.
- The intimidating buyer needs and wants to have an intelligent, tough, understanding salesman as a friend.
- Let him think the closing is his idea. The commission is all yours.

21

How to Close the Big Shooter

If any salesman is to rise head and shoulders above the crowd, he must know how to close the big shooter. Business is getting bigger and more complex each year. The salesman who wants a sizable piece of the pie today must be able to deal with educated, well-trained, sophisticated buyers. The chains and the giants are not the only ones who have such buyers. The successful independent enterprises doing a high dollar volume invariably have bright, competent buyers. Then there are the buying committees, boards of directors, advertising men and other management groups that the salesman often must work with as he closes sales with the big shooters. These people all think big. The salesman who expects to close a sale with the big shooters must think big, plan big, and close big.

The basics are essentially the same in closing a sale with the big shooter as with any other customer. The big shooter always expects and demands a high degree of expertise and performance from the sales-people who knock on his door. He has every right to entertain this attitude. The big shooter has much to offer the intelligent aggressive man who can help him to make more money and maintain his place of leadership.

When you objectively analyze it, you will see that what the big shooter wants and demands is the same thing that the experienced professional offers on every call: Product knowledge, industry know-how, latest developments, promotional ideas, sales help, and expert purchasing assistance. The chief difference is that you do it all on a grander scale, and sometimes in a more plush setting, as you close your sale with the big shooter.

DO YOUR HOMEWORK

If you are ill prepared on your first call to see the big shooter, you are in trouble. If you goof on your first interview, there will likely be a long dry spell before you get back in. Do your homework first. Here are some of the items you will want to determine prior to your first interview.

- Double check to be sure that you talk to the right man. There is no point in talking to someone who has no authority to buy.

- Don't try to go over anybody's head to get in to see Mr. Right Guy. If you do, you will have somebody fighting you every time you go back. Observe the firm's policy and go through the proper channels. Do use the imagination and the aggressiveness necessary. Go over a subordinate's head only as a last resort.

- Determine as closely as possible the volume of business the firm is doing. There are trade publications and reports in every business that can help you do this. Other salesmen, the Chamber of Commerce, and your own industry association, can help you. When you get an idea of the volume your prospect enjoys, you will be in a position to establish a quota for your first order.

- Learn everything you can about the personality of the buyer or buyers. Here is where your fellow salesmen can be of real help if they are already working with the big shooter.

- If you have a special promotion for the big shooter, practice and rehearse how you are going to lay it out for him. A buyer with a string of appointments each day can't afford to waste time with a salesman who fumbles. Avoid this by rehearsing your presentation ahead of time. Know what you are going to say and how you are going to say it.

- Practice the closing. Set yourself a goal and practice just how you plan to close. Rehearse until your confidence and enthusiasm can keep you in charge all the way.

- Be on time. Preferably arrive a bit early. Let the secretary know who you are and what time your appointment is. If she can work you in a little early she may do so. In any event, do not be five seconds late.

As you do your homework keep this in mind: The big shooter needs you. The bigger and busier the prospect, the more he appreciates competent, helpful salesmen who know how to close sales without wasting valuable time. He will know that you've done your homework well before you ask for the order the first time.

DON'T BE OVERAWED

When you operate in the big leagues don't be overawed. Though the place may reek with opulence and buzz with authority, it is inhabited by mortal businesspeople. They face the same problems each day that their smaller counterparts do. They are just as pleased to see a problem-solving, confident salesman as is the average customer you sell day by day. In fact, because of the sheer dollar volume at stake they are likely to hold a keener appreciation for the competent salesman who can save them time and money. You can capitalize on this sound truth and close sales that are astronomical by run-of-the-mill standards.

Benny Kitchens began his selling career with a New York based wholesaler. Benny's burning ambition was to be a manufacturer's representative on his own. After several years' experience, and while he was barely in his thirties, Benny formed his own agency. His specialty was bath and boutique merchandise. From the start Benny made a comfortable living. Yet he knew from experience and observation that he would have to sell some of the big shooters in order to reach his big money goals. He was aware, too, that selling the big shooter is good insurance. It not only enhances the manufacturer's representative's income, it assures him of the lines that he has and enables him to deal with new and progressive principals as his business expands.

Benny went after Kirkpatrick's, Inc., a group he had been unable to sell as a wholesaler salesman. In his new role as a direct mill representative he succeeded in setting up an interview thirty days ahead. The buyer's appointment schedule was tight and full for that long.

Benny already knew something about the prospect. He wisely spent time during the next thirty days learning as much more as he could about Kirkpatrick's, Inc. He prepared well, but he was still surprised at the thickness of the carpet on the floors and the rich decor of the offices. It added to his consternation to find three pairs of eyes instead of one coolly assessing him as he was ushered into the buyer's office.

Benny was in for another surprise. He quickly realized the buying committee was not out to dissect him. They were polished and courteous individuals. Obviously, they were shrewd businessmen intent on doing a job for their firm. Benny's experience helped him sense this. He forgot all else as he showed his samples, explained his deals, and invited comparisons. He ably fulfilled his role as an aggressive salesman prepared to make a contribution to the profit structure and the operation of a big shooter account. The basic selling technique served him well as his awe dissipated. Benny is no longer awe-struck when he earns a $5000 commission as he did on his first call on Kirkpatrick's, Inc. He learned in a hurry that the big shooters are no different from other viable businesspeople. They recognize and appreciate the value of a confident, determined salesman.

Forget any twinges of awe when you call on the big shooters. Concentrate on the closing as Benny Kitchens did. This is where the money is.

HOW TO BE READY FOR THE COMMITTEE

Selling the committee can be disconcerting to the novice. The novice may feel outnumbered and outmaneuvered. As an accomplished salesman you know that the basics remain the same as in a one-on-one situation. Practice your presentation diligently, polish and butter your sales talk, forget about the odds, and put your refined selling techniques on the line. A sale closed with the help of the big shooter's committee is worth all the concentration you can give it. It is surprisingly like many of the closed sales you tie down every day — only it's usually bigger and juicier.

HOW TO ANTICIPATE OBJECTIONS AND PRESSURES
FROM THE BIG SHOOTERS

A big part of getting ready for the big shooter is anticipating price objections and pressures for all the concessions the law allows. It's a matter of good business that you should anticipate that the buyer who gives you a million dollars worth of business is going to expect more from you than the buyer who offers you crumbs. Establish the best deal possible with the volume prices you can safely offer before you make your call.

When the big shooter asks you a question he wants a firm answer *now*. You can't do your homework in the big shooter's office and close your sale. If you have to phone your home office, your sales manager, or your principals every time a question arises, you will lose your man. He will be looking at his watch instead of listening to you.

Alvin Pence sells big shooters almost to the exclusion of all else. He is associated with a manufacturer of cook ware, kitchen utensils, and cutlery. His line is popularly priced high-volume merchandise particularly suited to today's mass merchandisers. Alvin anticipates objections and pressures. He has a lot of experience under his belt. Yet he always prepares diligently and methodically before he calls on a big shooter. Here is how Alvin goes about anticipating and preparing for objections and pressures that he has found to be a built-in part of closing sales with the big shooter. He puts it all down in black and white.

ALVIN PENCE'S PRE-CALL WORK SHEET

Name: Wonder Stores, Unlimited.
Buyers: Fred Sharpe and Guy Smartt.
Rating: AAA
Anticipated volume: $7,500,000 annually.
Selling plan:
1. Push special offer on blow-hard widgets.
2. Prepare a sales projection for each Wonder Stores outlet on blow-hard widgets.
3. Detail profit possible on blow-hard widgets for each outlet.
4. Show anticipated turnover per store.
5. Figure profit on each proposed initial order.
6. Call attention to the time limit on special offer and press for closing.
7. Be ready to explain that the special offer precludes any free goods if this question comes up.
8. Datings: Terms of extra 30 days can be granted if necessary.
9. Delivery: Two to three weeks on large orders. Fill-in orders will be expedited more quickly.

After making his preliminary outline — usually done on ruled legal paper — Alvin practices his presentation. He fills himself so full of what he is going to do that if an unexpected question or event pops up he is not thrown overboard.

It is sharp strategy to have the reserves that extra preparation will give you. When you fill yourself full of extra selling points and product knowledge, you can close your sale with the big shooter just as Alvin Pence does. The money he makes and the sales he closes do not come about by happenstance.

HOW TO TALK THE BIG SHOOTER'S LANGUAGE

It is puzzling, but I have found this to be an unfortunate truth: Many hard-working salesmen seem satisfied to sell only the small and medium sized accounts. Why would any salesman shy away from the big shooter? Is it "arithmetic fright?" Do the figures the big shooter is accustomed to use frighten some salesmen? Is it that the man who walks by this lucrative business is afraid that he will fall on his face if he tries to sell the big shooter?

There is simply no legitimate reason why a salesman with some experience and a mite of professional skill should bypass the big shooter. I have found that they are often easier to approach than the pee-wees and the marginal buyers. Frequently they are easier to sell because they have the ability and the training to recognize good deals and straightforward salesmen. Equally important, they have the capacity and the resources to place magnificent orders. Further, it is not difficult to talk the big shooter's language on an equal footing with him. This is what he wants. Here are pointers to insure that you can and do speak the big shooter's language as you close your sale.

- Raise your sights. Get into higher arithmetic. The big shooter isn't going to back off when you mention thousands of dollars. Realistically, he cannot afford to squander his time talking about penny-ante deals. His responsibilities are too great, his income too large, his expenses too high, and his business intellect too advanced, to think in small figures and weak profits. You can close a $500,000 sale with the big shooter a lot quicker than you can close a $1000 deal.

- Review the earlier section in this chapter "Don't Be Overawed." The big shooter wants to see you or you would never get near him. Grab this opportunity and close the sale much as you are accustomed to closing any sale. Only do it bigger and better. That is what the big shooter expects.

- Don't entertain thoughts of failure. If you do fail that is not the end of the ball game. All it means is that you must learn from the mistakes you made the first time. Revamp your sales plan, practice your stronger presentation, go back in and talk the pro's language. The big shooter will understand you and you can close your sale.

- Brush up your business vocabulary so that you can talk more than product knowledge. The big shooter doesn't buy merchandise to warehouse it. He buys it to resale at a fair profit. More than that, he wants it to move before it grows whiskers. If much of what he buys sits around too long, he is asked to do some uncomfortable explaining. You really speak the big shooter's language when you talk merchandising as you detail your product. Ideas — especially ideas on how to quickly move your product and add to your buyer's profit contribution — is talk he likes to hear. Use this technique along with other merchandising ideas your know-how and experience will uncover. You just might talk yourself into the fattest sale you ever closed. That's what the big shooter would like.

Kip Sadler knows that it pays to talk the big shooter's language. He remembers his first call on the home office of Beeman's, Inc., a subsidiary of a holding company specializing in the ownership of furniture and decorating outlets. Kip was trying to get his line of wicker furniture into Beeman's stores. On his first trip he told the buyer all about wicker furniture, but he failed to talk himself into a closed sale. That weekend he revamped his thinking and his presentation. When he went back a month later he spoke a different language.

On his second interview, which wasn't easy to set up, Kip opened by showing that any store doing a million dollars (he had determined that Beeman's stores all exceeded this figure) would easily sell $10,000 to $18,000 per month of his special furniture. He explained that this could be done on a special order basis. All each store had to do was invest $1000 in an opening display. Kip's company would pay the freight. The dealer could then use the no-cost handsome full color catalog for complete line sales of Kip's stock — chairs, tables, bars, stools, wood bins, and couches.

This time he talked the big shooter's language. He closed his sale for twenty display deals. At the end of six months his big shooter had rewarded him with $12,000 in commissions.

Kip says it's worth $2000 a month or more to be able to talk the big shooter's language. In his case he proved it.

HOW TO CLOSE THE BIG SHOOTER UNDER YOUR OWN POWER

As demanding as it is and as hot and heavy as the competition is for this most desirable business, you know that your closed sale with the big shooter is your baby. You may have some outside help and a few prayers in your behalf, but you know that, as in all sales you make, you are going to have to close the big shooter under your own power. Like all other independent, ambitious salesmen, this is exactly the way you want it.

Let's review a few of the basics involved in the closing of the big shooter. Add the techniques and ideas your own initiative will bring to light. Study this whole chapter carefully and keep your power hot. The following ideas are in addition to the strategies already discussed. When you call on the big shooters:

- **Hang loose. Be flexible.**
  Don't go in with your mind so strapped by a canned presentation that you cannot roll with the punches. When you have studied your prospect and practiced your presentation, don't get uptight. If you are unceremoniously interrupted, don't get flustered. Be ready, act ready, when the unexpected happens.

- **Keep control.**
  We can't emphasize this too often. Keep control of every sales interview. It is mandatory in the super-charged presence of the big shooters. These gentlemen are notoriously intolerant of faltering salesmen. They do not have time to waste.

- **Pick a lead item for a foothold.**
  This may be a special promotion, a hot price, or a new product. It is better to have an exciting lead-in than to dump everything in front of the big shooter and hope he picks something out. These buyers are not inclined to do your work for you.

- **Keep yourself well-informed.**
  The big shooter always wants to know "what is new." Be a reference catalog for him. He will help you close your sale because he will want you to come back.

- **Be enthusiastic.**
  Don't let the icy efficiency of the big shooter's office put a chill on your enthusiasm. The big shooter is influenced by a salesman's enthusiastic attitude just as is any other warm-blooded businessman.

- **Be credible.**
  The big shooter won't touch any salesman with a ten foot pole if he can't believe him.

- **Welcome resistance.**
  Objections, questions, resistance, all indicate interest. Welcome it as a good omen. As long as you have prepared well, you can turn these into selling advantages, as we have pointed out in this book.

- **Ask for the order.**
  The big shooter isn't looking for a conversationalist or an entertainer. He knows you are there for an order. Don't disappoint him. Ask for the order.

PURVES' INSTANT POINTERS ON HOW TO CLOSE
THE BIG SHOOTER

- You have to close the big shooter to get in the upper brackets of the selling profession.
- Do your homework. If you goof in your first interview you may suffer a long dry spell before you get back in.
- Don't be overawed by the big shooter. He has a keen appreciation of the competent salesman.
- Forget about the odds when you face the big shooters' buying committee. Concentrate on the job you came to do.
- Anticipate and prepare for objections and pressures as you face the big shooter.
- Don't bypass the big shooter. There is too much at stake. Talk his language and close your sale.
- Close the big shooter under your own power. The closed sale is your baby.

22

Ten Techniques to Speed Up the Closing Process

The closing of the sale is not the tail on the dog. It is not a separate part of the sales interview to be tacked on after everything else has been said and done. The closing is an integral part of the sales interview. It is the warp and the woof. It is the beginning and the end.

The first word of your sales presentation should be directed at the closing. Each step should logically lead to the closing. The closing can come at the beginning, in the middle, or any place and at any time during an exciting, compelling sales endeavor. It need not bring up the rear.

ASK FOR THE ORDER QUICK AND OFTEN

Volumes have been written about the "right time to close." I have a tried and true theory regarding this: The "right time to close" is at the first opportunity. The right time to ask for the order is at the first signal that the customer is ready. If in doubt as to whether the customer is ready, there is a sure-fire way to find out—ask for the order quick and often. If the customer isn't fully prepared to say yes when you ask early in the presentation, you are not out of steam. You can go ahead with your selling plan until you see another flick of interest. When you do, ask for the order again. This way you are assured of closing your sale as soon as possible.

Emory Karnes began his sales career early as a door to door salesman selling sewing machines. He was required to learn a canned presentation. His manager told him that once he learned the whole thing his future was assured. All Emory had to do, he said, was to use his literature and go through the entire process word by word. Then when he had recited all his memorized sales talk his closed sale would fall into his lap.

It didn't quite work out that way. Emory did not sell his first machine until he learned on his own. What he learned was that he was putting his prospects to sleep with his parrot-like sales pitch. He sold his first machine when he abandoned his rote method and looked for a closing sign. It came early. He sold his first machine when he was only five minutes into his sales talk. His prospect asked a question that indicated interest. Emory answered and asked for the order. Emory has had his own sales organization for a long time now. The first thing he teaches new trainees is to ask for the order quick and often. He discovered long ago that this is one fine technique to speed up the closing of the sale.

The beginning and the end of your sales presentation are the most important parts. And they need not be far apart. You know to get off to a fast, attention-grabbing start. Do not decide you can't close until you have reached a predetermined point. Be prepared to close as quickly as your prospect is ready.

There is a story of a young politician who asked an old campaigner what he thought of a speech the young man had just proudly delivered.

"Well, son," said the old politician candidly, "your beginning was commanding, your ending was majestic, but there was too much middle. That's where you lost 'em—right in the middle."

The same thing can happen to your sale if you fail to ask for the order quick and often. You can lose it right in the middle if the customer is ready to close early and never gets the opportunity.

KEEP ON TARGET

One of the best ways to keep on target is to use the ABC technique when you are in pursuit of an exciting sale. I don't remember where or when I first heard of the ABC system, but I highly recommend it to you. Here is the ABC method: *Always Be Closing.*

Wrap your entire presentation around the closed sale. Anything else is a monumental waste of time. Unless the sale is closed your customer gains nothing and you lose all.

Lynda Hilt has an enviable record of closed sales. Invariably she sells more homes than her next two competitors. She employs the ABC technique daily. Her first step is to qualify her prospect. This is her first closing step. She knows that she can't close a sale with a bankrupt prospect.

Her next closing step is the first area of agreement. She keeps right on target. If the prospect likes a big yard, she calls attention to this feature and asks for the order. If the prospect doesn't buy on the first appeal she stays on track to the next. "Look at that fireplace," she will say. "Gee, I would like to come over and have a cup of coffee with you right in front of a glowing fire in this lovely room. You want a fireplace. Don't you think we had better sign a purchase agreement now and take this house off the market before somebody else gets it?"

Lynda never strays. She makes notes on what her prospect wants. When she finds one such feature she tries for the close. Her record of closed sales proves her logic is sound. She wastes no time.

Put the ABC technique to work whatever you are selling. *Always Be Closing.* This can't help but speed up the whole undertaking.

GIVE YOUR CUSTOMER A CHANCE

Speeding up the closing is not a spectator sport. Your customer does not want to be a bystander, he wants to be involved. If he is going to spend his money give him a chance to take part.

Give your customer a chance—

- **To ask questions.**
  Give your customer a chance to ask questions. Don't ignore his questions or treat them lightly. No matter how inconsequential they may seem to you, each question is a serious matter to him. If you do not treat the customer or prospect's question with respect, he will be offended and you will lose him. Common courtesy dictates that you give your customer's questions every consideration. There is one overriding reason for you to listen carefully: Questions spell customer interest. They are loaded with signals that can speed the closing of your sale.
- **To Talk.**
  It's not much of a sales presentation when the salesman does all of the talking. If the customer has no chance to talk how will you know what he is thinking? When you know what your customer is thinking you can shape your presentation to take advantage of the closing signals his thoughts shoot out. Give your customer a chance to talk. He can speed up the closing of your sale for you.
- **To make objections.**
  No disinterested customer bothers to make objections. When a customer or prospect raises an objection, he isn't trying to put you down. He is saying, "Hey, I'm interested, but I want you to clear up something for me."
  Give your customer a chance to make objections. If you don't know what his objections are you may never erase them. When

you give him a chance to make objections, they are in the open where you can deal with them and speed up the closing process.

- **To get involved.**
  Give your customer a chance to get involved. Invite him to help you with your demonstration, urge him to handle your product, to check your figures, make comparisons, and be active in your presentation. The two of you can get the job done in a hurry.

- **To say yes.**
  Ask for the order—ask for the order—ask for the order. Give your customer a chance to say yes. This is the best device yet invented to speed up the closing.

HOW TO BE READY FOR A NO AND GET A YES

When you are ready you can anticipate a no and get a yes. As an experienced salesman you are keenly aware that an occasional no is a natural part of the closing process. Of course the way to be ready for a no is to fill yourself so full of your subject that you will automatically have a reservoir of potent sales points to shunt aside the no's and move your customer nearer the close. You can use the abundance of ideas we have covered in this book to thoroughly prepare yourself for a no. Then you will be ready to brush it aside and use the refined selling techniques at your fingertips to get a yes. In this case a no won't slow you down as you push on to a speedy closing.

SHUN THE COMPLICATED

The salesman who gets himself bogged down in trivia and unnecessary detail cannot hope to effect a speedy closing. Shun the complicated. Use and say only what will move your sale toward a quick close. Anything else is a stumbling block—shun it like the plague. Keep your presentation clean and simple. Your customer will show appreciation by saying yes early. You shun the complicated when you plan what you are going to do, rehearse what you plan to say, and perfect it all with diligent practice. This practically guarantees that your closing will be right on time.

WORK THE HOT BUTTON

The hot button is whatever interests your customer most. He may like several things about your product or proposition, but in nearly every case there is one appeal about your product or idea that is stronger than any other. This is the hot button. As soon as you have identified it, hammer it repeatedly. Bring the discussion back to that item at every opportunity. Each time you steer your customer or prospect back to the hot button ask for the order. The hot button can speed up your closing.

Ira Meyer shows and sells quarter horses in the western states. He had a price tag of $51,000 on one of his blue ribbon winners. The horse was a big stallion aptly named My Pride. A Mr. H.K. Lathrop came to Ira Meyer's stables to buy a "winner," as he put it. He was fascinated by My Pride, but rebelled at the $51,000 price. Ira hit the hot button by handing Mr. Lathrop about two dozen cups and ribbons My Pride had won. Mr. Lathrop balked. Too much money, he said. Ira brought out recent newspaper clippings showing him happily accepting prize money My Pride had won the month before. Ira was hitting the hot button. While Mr. Lathrop was holding the clipping, Mrs. Lathrop said, "Dear, you have wanted a pedigreed winner for a long time. Why don't you buy that beautiful animal?" Ira worked the hot button again by pointing out that this indeed was a remarkable prize winning horse, and one he parted with reluctantly. He could truly appreciate the satisfaction Mr. Lathrop would experience as the proud owner of such a magnificent show horse. "Now is the time to buy," said Ira. "Tomorrow could be too late."

Hitting the hot button over and over quickly closed the deal. Mr. Lathrop is now showing My Pride, and Ira has $51,000 to spend as he pleases. When you hit the hot button and speed up the closing of your sale, everybody gets what they want when they should have it— including you.

TELL AND RETELL

Telling and retelling is to emphasize and dramatize selling points. The human mind responds to repetition. Telling and retelling the main features of your sales presentation will make a solid impression on your customer's mind. Mentioning a key feature only once may momentarily get his attention. Telling and retelling him about it makes it important and plants the idea in his thinking.

The value of telling and retelling is delightfully illustrated by the story of the barely literate old preacher who had great success at winning souls. After a particularly successful evangelistic revival service, one of his more polished associates marvelled, "Reverend, what is the secret of your sermons? How do you win so many converts at your meetings?"

The old preacher explained, "Well, first I tells 'em what I'm gonna tell 'em, next I tells 'em, then I tells 'em what I done told 'em."

Tell and retell 'em. It will speed up your closing.

HOW TO KEEP AND USE CUSTOMER RECORDS TO SPEED UP THE CLOSING

Salesmen generally have a notorious dislike for paper work. That is, a salesman dislikes paper work until he recognizes that it will speed up the closing of many of his sales. Veteran salesmen seldom fly by the seat of their pants. Qualified sales executives insist that their salesmen keep complete customer records. These men know from experience that customer records are essential to quick closings.

Customer records should contain such vital statistics as:

Full company name
Buyer's name
Name of buyer's secretary
Buying hours
Full address
Phone number
Customer classification
Credit rating

Notes should be recorded on the record sheet or index card used for individual customer records before the first call. These notes should cover the item or items you plan to sell on this call. All ideas you intend to use should be jotted on the record. Then just before you go in to see your customer or client you can refresh your memory and prime yourself for a quick closing.

After the first call, and on each succeeding call, you should make notes on everything that transpired on the call—what you sold, what you failed to sell, what the customer liked or didn't like, plus anything you deem helpful to future calls. Naturally you will want to make notes to show anything that sparked interest for reference when you make your next call. File your customer record cards or sheets so that you can easily lay your hands on this information to close your next sale. I like to use 3 × 5 index cards. I file them alphabetically by towns so that I can pull the cards and plan my closing strategy for each customer or prospect in the area. This eliminates guesswork, saves time, and streamlines the closing of many sales.

HOW TO CLOSE BY CONTRAST

Often when you are closing your sale against stiff competition you can speed up your closing by the adroit use of contrast. To contrast, in this sense, means to compare or appraise in respect to differences. The differences can be in the product itself, in the stability or history of competing firms, in delivery performance, in warranties, in advertising policies, pricing, stocking inventories, or any of a multitude of factors which can and do influence the consummation of a sale. When you have a selling advantage you can dramatically take advantage of it by comparing or contrasting it with the competitor's product or performance. When you support your sales points with obvious advantages portrayed by a contrast, you have an open door to a closed sale. There can be no better time to ask for the order.

Alvin Spooner is a quick-witted salesman who works for a large packer of fruit. He covers a wide area calling on wholesalers, private label franchisers, chains, and institutions. He closed a sale for three trailer loads of sliced peaches this year to a private label distributor. He used the contrast technique to get the job done. Here's how:

Alvin demonstrated his product to the buying committee by opening a tin of his peaches. He used plastic spoons and had all three members of the committee taste the product. He called attention to the uniformity of the fruit, the distinctive color, and the pleasing aroma. The committee unanimously agreed that Alvin did indeed have a fine product. But, they complained, the price was too high. They were buying a similar product for 10% less money. Well, closing a sale by contrast involves a comparison of similar objects to set off their dissimilar qualities. Alvin's long experience stood him in good stead. He asked for a number ten tin (3 quarts) of his competitor's product. He insisted on paying his customer for this sample. Then he went to his car and brought in another tin of the same size of his product. He opened each tin and carefully drained the syrup and juice off the peaches. Next he showed the buyers the amount of fruit that was left. Alvin's product had at least a third more of good solid fruit in the opened tin. All that was left to do was ask for the order. This experienced salesman lost no time in doing that. He closed his sale with the contrast technique, collected his four figure commission, and is now supplying this profitable volume account with a variety of his products.

Use the contrast method to point up the unique advantages and benefits you can offer your customer or prospect. It is a powerful tool to speed up the closing of a sale.

HOW TO RECOGNIZE "TIME TO CLOSE" SIGNALS

The salesman who knows how to recognize "time to close" signals can speed up the closing process on practically any sale. The reason is simple. He will try for the close at the first signal.

Basically there are two kinds of closing signals: Voluntary and involuntary. Any comments or questions by the customer or prospect are voluntary signals that it is time to close the sale. For example, if a customer asks, "How do I have to pay for it?" or "What kind of terms do you have?" that is a closing signal that shouts "Hey, I'm ready to buy." If you ignore such voluntary signals and push on with more detail your customer may lose interest and you will lose the sale.

When a customer shoots out signals by asking questions or making comments such as, "How long will it take to get delivery," "I really prefer this model," or "Yes, I like that idea," don't go ahead with your presentation. Ask for the order then and there. It is time to close your sale.

Involuntary closing signals may be a little harder to recognize, but they are just as valid as are the more obvious voluntary signals. To detect them you should be alert for such signs of interest as these: The customer or prospect leans forward in his chair, he suddenly becomes more relaxed and friendly, his attitude becomes positive, the tone of his voice changes, he makes an objection such as, "That's a hot deal, but my inventory is so heavy I ought not to buy."

When you catch such signals try for the close. If you are premature, go on with your presentation and add more value. Try at each signal until the sale is closed.

Experience will give you a sort of sixth sense. Many successful salesmen cannot tell you exactly how they recognize an involuntary closing signal. Yet they develop an insight that enables them to recognize the exact moment to close a sale. Watch for closing signals. The better you become at recognizing them, the more you can speed up the closing process.

PURVES' INSTANT POINTERS ON TECHNIQUES
TO SPEED UP THE CLOSING PROCESS

- The closing of the sale is not the tail on the dog.
- The "right time to close" is at the first opportunity.

- Ask for the order quick and often.
- Wrap your entire presentation around the closed sale.
- Speeding up the closing is not a spectator sport.
- Shun the complicated.
- Work the hot button.
- Tell and retell.
- Use customer records to speed up the closing.
- The use of contrast can speed your closing.
- The better you are at recognizing closing signals, the better you can speed up the closing process.

23

How to Make Sure the Sale Stays Closed

It is a crushing experience to have a sale cancelled. It need not happen. Except in the rarest of cases, there was really no sale in the first place if it was cancelled once the salesman got out of sight. When a sale is made in good faith there should be no loose ends left to come unravelled. The customer and the salesman should each have a clear understanding of everything that was agreed to. It is the salesman's responsibility to make sure that the customer understands every part of the agreement. When both parties are in accord there can be no legitimate reason for a sale that does not stay closed.

Yet is has happened. When the closed sale evaporates it leaves the salesman feeling as lonely as a long distance runner. This need not happen to you. Here are some steps to insure that your closed sale stays closed.

COMPLIMENT THE CUSTOMER ON HIS GOOD JUDGMENT

The smart salesman makes his customer feel smart. When you make your customer feel smart your sale will stay closed. When you have put together a mutually profitable package and sold it (the smart salesman will sell no other), you have plenty of reason to compliment your customer on his good judgment. For instance:

- If you have sold him merchandise which he will resell, you can compliment him on his keen money sense. Do this by again pointing out the money he can expect to make from his first purchase. Tell him that you realize that he has considered the profit he will make again and again as your merchandise turns for him. Compliment him by saying that it is his good judgment in money matters that keeps him ahead of the competition.

- Compliment him on the money he has saved by buying the right merchandise at the right price. If he has second thoughts after you leave, the money he has saved will keep your sale closed. No right-thinking businessman will want to void a good buy where extra profit can be made.

- Say "we" when you reaffirm your customer's good judgment. When you say "We are both going to be glad about this deal," your customer will identify with you. When you say "We will be doing business together a long time," for example, he will feel that you are on his side. The customer is complimented when a sincere and able salesman lets him know that he (the salesman) appreciates the close bond that always exists between a loyal customer and a helpful salesman.

- When you compliment your customer's good judgment after the sale is closed, don't be a chatterbox. Too much of a good thing is tiresome. Compliment him briefly, warmly, matter-of-factly, and then get out.

GET THE ORDER SIGNED

Salesmen write orders every day for old friends and never ask them to sign the order. When you know your customer, and have the utmost faith in him due to a long, happy association, it is not necessary to insist on a signed order except in unusual cases. There are salesmen and sales managers who won't agree with this assessment. Nevertheless, my own experience justifies my reasoning. But if there is the slightest doubt in your mind, the smallest hint of trouble, by all means get your order signed. The fickle buyer who gets cold feet and mistrusts his own judgment is slower about cancelling a closed sale if he has signed the order. Play it safe. When your business sense or intuition says, "Get the order signed," then by all means get it signed.

I always get orders signed on new accounts. I follow this procedure until the customer and I thoroughly know and understand each other. In any event, always hand your customer his copy of the order. Of course, if the customer's firm uses their own P.O. forms you will be handed a copy. When all parties have a firm copy of the purchase agreement the sale is not a fuzzy deal which could come unglued.

Get the order signed when your firm's policy is to get all orders signed. Get the order signed when your customer wants it that way (some orders require the salesman's signature along with the buyer's).

Get the order signed in every case where there is an indication that it will keep the closed sale closed.

HANDLE THE ORDER WITH CARE

Closing a sale is an earnest matter for the buyer. Few things irritate a buyer more than a salesman who is flippant or one who treats a sale lightly. Usually a salesman who indulges in such gross behavior is immature or is trying to hide the intense pressure he feels. Whatever the reason, the customer will not be favorably impressed when this mistake is made. As an experienced, aggressive salesman, and as a business man, you will handle every sale with the care and respect it deserves. A sale closed in this atmosphere will stay closed.

HOW TO TIE YOUR CLOSED SALE DOWN
BY RESTATING KEY POINTS

When your sale is closed you can tie it down securely by briefly restating key points. Don't make the complete presentation all over again. Hit the high spots only.

Jerry Shoemaker, a salesman in the Midwest, recently wrote a huge order for a Christmas toy. His customer was a well-known family enterprise that had dominated the variety and discount business in their town for generations. As soon as Jerry had his order he tied down his closed sale by restating these key points:

- Jerry verified the November first delivery date.
- Confirmed that the toy would be in assorted colors.
- Emphasized the safety features of the toy.
- Made note again that it was safe and laboratory approved.
- Recalled that it was lightweight so that the child could handle it easily.
- Called attention again to the toy's durable structure.
- Showed again that the toy was adjustable.
- Again stressed that the toy was highly profitable.
- Reread the co-op advertising agreement.
- Assured the customer that there would be back-up stock.

It took Jerry thirty minutes to get the order. He spent only three minutes restating the key points. It was enough to tie down his closed sale.

Make your recap short and succinct. It is never a good idea to dally around unnecessarily after you have your closed sale. It's a bigger mistake to leave before the sale is safely under wraps.

HOW TO USE YOUR DEPARTURE
TO MAKE SURE THE SALE STAYS CLOSED

You have closed an important sale under tough conditions. You feel the strain and tension. This is the time to keep a tight check on your emotions and on what you do and say. Here are a few things to watch. There are others, but two or three will give you the idea.

- Don't make it obvious that you are elated to have done the job. This could convey the impression that a big order is a rare thing for you.
- Don't be too effusive. Thank your customer and then turn the conversation into other channels, such as the improved delivery and shipping system your firm is arranging because of growing business and a desire to give the best possible service.
- Do thank the customer in a friendly and unhurried manner. Use such remarks as, "Thank you for the order, Mr. Customer. I'll phone this in today and get your order on its way," or "You will make some money on this deal, Mr. Customer. I'll see you on my next trip. And thank you again."
- As a rule, the salesman should be the one to bring the interview to a quick, friendly close as soon as the sale is closed. There are exceptions, but they will be easily recognized if there is a reason to linger. Take your closed sale and get out unless you *know* your customer wants you to hang around for a good reason. A friendly, dignified departure can do much to make sure that the sale which you have just closed stays closed.

HOW TO CHECK ON THE ORDER TO MAKE SURE
THAT THE SALE STAYS CLOSED

It has been said that service is one more overworked word in the lexicon of business. There is probably considerable truth to this theory, but a customer still expects reasonable service from his salesman. And rightfully so. Even though the mills that my sales agency represents have WATS numbers, I still get a lot of calls on weekends when my customers know that I am home. If the customer wants an order in a hurry he will often call me and enlist my help. If the customer has any problems or special requests it is only natural that he will look to his salesman. I find, as I'm sure many of my peers do, that staying on top of the order is good insurance. It keeps the sale closed. Customers love a willing trouble shooter.

Cordis Payne had sold a large order to a gift and novelty house located in a popular resort area. The first heavy weekend for the resort was traditionally Decoration Day weekend. Cordis' customer had been emphatic in insisting that delivery be made at least one week prior to Decoration Day. On May first when Cordis had received no invoice copy or other indication that shipment had been effected, he called his plant. When he was told that shipment had been made the day before he asked for the name of the carrier and the waybill number. He had no sooner hung up the phone than Shamrock Holiday Gifts called him demanding to know what happened to their order. Because of his forethought Cordis was able to give specific assurance that the order was on its way and would arrive ahead of the one week deadline. He gave his customer the carrier's name and waybill number so that he could call the local terminal if the need arose. As it was the goods were delivered by May seventh with time to spare.

Cordis saved his $1700 commission by keeping his sale closed. Checking on the order is good business insurance. It keeps sales closed, it keeps customers happy, and it brings commissions home safely.

HOW TO USE CREDIT INFORMATION TO MAKE SURE THAT YOUR SALE STAYS CLOSED

Another way to insure your closed sale is to make certain that you can deliver the goods after you have made the sale. You can deliver your goods or services only if your customer has the resources and the heart to pay as agreed. Otherwise there is not point in pursuing the sale at all. Salesmen are not paid on the basis of the orders they write. They are paid on the basis of goods or services sold and delivered.

When selling a customer for the first time it is essential that you obtain complete credit information. Unless you are working for Santa Claus your credit manager will insist on this much. Most customers—the strong ones almost without exception—will cooperate in providing the needed information. On many occasions I have been handed a financial statement and trade references along with the initial purchase order. When the information has not been volunteered it is easy enough to ask for it. Your buyers are business people. They appreciate that you need to know their banking connections, their trade references, and their financial condition, in order to ship a high figure order.

New customers are not the only ones who must be sound in order for you to get your closed sale delivered. The rule applies to old friends as well as new. When an account is dragging its feet and missing discounts, the only way to make sure that your closed sale stays closed is to collect any past due monies.

There is no reason to feel squeamish as you use credit information to make sure that your sale stays closed. Asking for credit information is like asking for the order: You don't really have a closed sale until you get both.

PROMISE WHAT YOU CAN DELIVER AND
DELIVER WHAT YOU PROMISE

It would seem that it is so obvious that you must promise only what you can deliver and deliver what you promise that no salesman would ever deviate from this maxim. As all professionals know, the pressures of the market place are enormous. The professionals know that an unkept promise will destroy a closed sale. Only an unprofessional man tormented by moral bankruptcy will make business promises he cannot keep. If a salesman should succumb to such an inexcusable weakness his closed sale will not stay closed and his customers will vanish.

A friend of mine told me of his experience with a misguided salesman and the agony of cancelled sales caused by his abnormal selling techniques. T.K. (Bud) Licklider had hired a new salesman. Bud's house specialized in selling fabrics which were off goods, distressed, or drops. Due to the nature of the goods they were sold at below normal prices. Each salesman for Bud's firm represented the goods honestly. Business was always such that it was hard to keep up with the demand. Despite this, Bud's maverick salesman couldn't play it straight. He sold the goods as perfects and running lines with continuity. The new man never made the second trip through his territory. The cost of adjustments, allowances, freight on returned orders, and the loss of goodwill on sales that didn't stay closed, dictated that his services be terminated.

As an experienced and upright salesman you know that no firm and no salesman can survive closed sales sacrificed in such an unconscionable manner. Your closed sale will stay closed when you promise what you can deliver and deliver what you promise. Your social intelligence and your personal code of ethics will prohibit anything less.

BE AVAILABLE AFTER THE SALE IS CLOSED

Industrial salesmen and any other salesmen selling a complicated machine or device expect to be called upon for advice and help. Such a sale normally involves much money. The salesman is expected to be around to render service and offer advice to his customers after the sale is closed. Whatever you are selling it is excellent policy to keep in touch after the sale is made. This affords the salesman the opportunity to straighten out any problems or misunderstandings before his closed sale is jeopardized. The salesman who assumes the attitude that his responsibility ends when the sale is closed suffers from a poverty of heart that can be costly.

Naturally the amount of time a salesman spends with a customer after the sale is closed must be balanced against his selling time. Be available after the order is closed, but don't devote so much time to it that you miss other closed sales because you are not in the field. We all want to keep our sale closed, but we all must keep closing other sales too.

HOW TO GET OTHERS
TO HELP KEEP YOUR SALE CLOSED

Once your sale is closed what happens to it is dependent upon any number of people. The billing department, the warehouse crew, the shipping department, the deliveryman, the office manager, the switchboard operator, and the credit department, are among those who can impede or expedite an order. If at all possible it is well for the salesman to know these people. If you build a reservoir of goodwill with your co-workers they will remember you. And because they like you and consider you a friend they will give your closed sale every consideration as it passes through their hands. In other words, they can help keep your closed sale closed.

I know of one salesman who represents a soft goods mill in the south. His orders always seem to get high priority. I have never heard him complain of slow delivery or haphazard billing as I have heard some of his friends do. I have learned his secret. He keeps a record of the birthday of every employee in the mill; when an employee has a birthday he knows that Roy is going to send him a birthday greeting with a little

personal note included. Twice a year when all the sale
for semi-annual meetings, Roy updates his list an
employees to it. This little gesture spurs the help of ab
keeping Roy's sales closed.

You don't have to wine and dine your co-workers t
you keep your sale closed. Besides keeping on frienc
with them, you can always double check each order t
plainly written and thoroughly legible. The full addre
along with credit information, routing, and a compl
sizes, colors, assortments, or any detail concerning ⟶o items on the
order. When you are careful with your order the other people who handle it will be more likely to treat it with care. This helps keep the sale
closed.

Avoid anything that may smack of politics or overt socializing when
seeking your co-worker's help to keep your sale closed. If you are
crudely currying favor to get preferential treatment, it will backfire.
Keep everything done on behalf of your closed sale above board and on
a business basis. This can be done warmly and effectively. It is the only
way to do it if you value the help of your co-workers in keeping your
closed sale closed.

HOW TO LOCK IN YOUR CLOSED SALE
WHEN IT IS MADE

The best time to take steps to make sure that your sale stays closed is
when you close it. Here are a number of steps which you can utilize to
lock in your closed sale as you make it.

- **Clarify any guarantees or warranties.**
  There can be a lot of unnecessary ill feelings over guarantees and
  warranties which are implied or explicit. If the product you are selling carries a warranty, don't blow it up in order to close a sale. If
  you do, it may come home to haunt you, and you may lose your
  commission and your customer. The buyer has a tendency to put a
  liberal and generous interpretation on a warranty. Of necessity the
  manufacturer's interpretation is limited to exactly what is in
  print. Explain the limitations and the reason for them even as you
  emphasize the selling points of the warranty. This will sharply
  reduce later misunderstandings that could wipe out your closed
  sale.

- **Clarify your returned goods policy.**
  Unless you are placing consigned merchandise your merchandise should not be returned if it measures up to acceptable standards. Occasionally a large customer will threaten the supplier with a loss of business if his unreasonable demands for return privileges are not met. Too, a customer who has insisted on a bigger purchase than the salesman suggested can sometimes scream bloody murder if his optimism proves to be faulty. My own feeling is that a sale is not a closed sale if the door is left open to return the goods indiscriminately. The buyer as well as the seller has contractual obligations and neither should seek an unfair advantage over the other. You can explain your firm's policy regarding returns without making a federal case out of it, or without alarming anybody. Your customer knows that a deal is a deal. He is a businessman. Clarify any questions regarding returned goods at the time of the closing. Then your closed sale won't fly apart if your customer doesn't move it all the day he gets it. Rather, he will do as any smart operator should: Put on a sales campaign of his own and move the merchandise at a fair profit.
- **Make certain the pricing agreement is understood.**
  If you have a firm price, well and good. Insert it clearly on your order pad as you close your sale. If the merchandise is to be priced at time of availability, be sure your customer understands this. Put it in writing so that your closed sale won't be shot down later.
- **Explain the credit terms.**
  If your closed sale carries net 30 terms, indicate this. If it carries terms of 2% 10 days or 2% 30 days write this in your order. Don't leave the terms space blank. Your customer may expect more than you can give if this is left to his imagination. And like any misunderstanding, this can endanger your closed sale. You lock in your sale by leaving nothing to your customer's imagination.
- **Leave a copy of the order.**
  After you have carefully filled in all the detailed and pertinent information on your order, leave a copy with your customer. Both of you are entitled to a copy. A sale is a contractual business agreement. As such, a fully documented record should be filed by all parties concerned. One important aspect of this is that your customer can refer to his copy of the order if a question crosses his mind. A copy of the order in the hands of your customer can erase doubts, answer questions, and keep your sale closed.

PURVES' INSTANT POINTERS ON HOW TO MAKE SURE
YOUR SALE STAYS CLOSED

- Compliment the customer on his good judgment.
- The smart salesman makes his customer feel smart.
- Get the order signed.
- Handle the order with care.
- Tie down your closed sale by restating key points.
- A friendly, dignified departure can help keep your sale closed.
- Check on the progress of the order to make sure your sale stays closed.
- Full credit information with the order can keep your sale closed.
- Promise what you can deliver and deliver what you promise.
- Be available after the sale is closed.
- Enlist the help of your co-workers to keep your sale closed.
- The ideal time to lock in your closed sale is when you write the order.

24

Ten Closing Keys That Can Explode Your Closing Power

The more explosive your closing power the more sales you will close. Further, when your closing power is strong you waste no time in getting the job done. A good salesman is always a strong closer and a strong closer is always a good salesman.

Every step that you take in selling from prospecting to handling objections is focused on one goal—the closed sale. If the sale is not closed, all else is an exercise in futility.

A strong closer is confident in every step of the sale. He knows where he is going and he knows how to get there. On the other hand, the salesman who has misgivings about his closing abilities is miserably handicapped. He actually dreads the time to close. He cannot appreciate how many sales are closed simply because the salesman is programmed to ask for and expect the order.

As an experienced fire-balling salesman you are fully cognizant of the importance of being a powerful closer. You work at it constantly. Here are ten closing keys that can explode your closing power. Put them to work today and watch your closed sales and your income explode.

KEY #1: START CLOSING AT THE FIRST CONTACT

As you design and practice your sales presentation eliminate all the gingerbread. Anything that fails to move your customer or prospect toward the closing is so much fluff. The first words of your presentation should be constructed to grab and hold the buyer's attention.

From the start the customer wants to know what he is going to get out of the deal. Get into customer benefits at once. Get your customer involved as his excitement and anticipation grow. Avoid the frills. Leap from peak to peak as you employ the prime selling features of your product or proposition. Do not get bogged down in detail. If you do, this will put your customer in a state of somnolence. Keep him awake and riding high with you by the use of questions, by having him handle and examine your product, by demonstrating the essential truth of what you are saying, and by dramatically illustrating and proving key points.

Jim Sallee, a New Mexico salesman, recalls how a druggist customer unwittingly taught him the importance of starting the closing at the beginning of the sale. Jim had a new line of storage files he was sure the druggist needed. He spent the first fifteen minutes describing the files and showing the literature that he had brought in with him. The busy druggist stopped him with, "Son, why don't you tell me how to use them and when I can get them?"

Jim did and the druggist bought. Jim says that since that day he has started every sales presentation with a quick closing in mind. Today he is sales manager for a large office supply house. As such, one of his chief responsibilities is guiding and training the sales force. He drills into each man the explosive power of beginning the closing at the first contact. This technique keeps his men and his firm on the top shelf.

Use this key as Jim does. It can explode your closing power and your earnings.

KEY #2: HOW TO USE OBJECTIONS
TO MAKE A POWER PLAY

Experienced salesmen count objections as a part of the closing process. Keep in mind that when you are in the process of closing a sale you are asking somebody to do something. The almost immediate reaction is a defensive attitude. The prospect or customer is going to have to make a decision. He is going to have to take action. It is easier to make no decision. It is easier to take no action. So the buyer raises an objection. It is normal. It is a good omen.

The novice may not be able to cope with an objection. The veteran proficient salesman expects and welcomes expressed objections. When the prospect or customer raises an objection, he gives the salesman a clue as to what to do next to move the sale nearer to the closing

Here are two examples that can generate ideas that will enable you to use the objections key to explode your personal closing power.

- One of the best trap closings is based on an objection. It works like this: When the prospect or customer is harping on one objection, whatever it may be, the salesman says, "If we can get that objection out of the way is there any reason why we can't close this deal right now?" Or he might phrase it thus: "As I understand it, if we can get this objection out of the way we can close this deal here and now. Right?"

When the customer responds affirmatively to this question he has committed himself. All that is left for the salesman to do is to remove the objection and close the sale. Of course, no salesman should ask this question unless he is prepared to deal with the objection promptly. But that is what closing sales is about.

The clincher in this technique is to be sure to insert that time limit "now" in your question. If you don't get a commitment to close "now"—as soon as the objection is put to rest—you may be hit right between the horns with another objection that zips in from the thin cold air of nowhere. For instance, if the objection is because of price and you manage to arrange a price concession but fail to insert the "now" clause, look out! A little red devil flares up in the buyer's mind and says, "Hey, if I got that price through one little old objection, maybe I can get another by laying it on a little heavier."

Use objections to make a power play to close your sale. Protect yourself and your closed sale as you do by inserting an action clause.

- "The Standing Room Only" technique is a reliable way to use objections to make a power play. Buyers are only human. They don't want to miss any opportunities. Above all, they don't want the competition to get something they can't get.

When you have a special deal don't let it be a special that lasts forever. Make it special when the buyer procrastinates. Say, "Mr. Customer, I may not have this deal tomorrow. Take advantage of it now." Or, "Mr. Customer, buy this deal today. Tomorrow it will be back up to the regular price and will cost you $250 more."

When you use the SRO technique to make a power play, do so in a subtle manner. If the salesman is a bit crude it may not work. This technique should (like all closing techniques) be used honestly and truthfully. If you have been in the field long enought to establish a reputation for credibility, this is a most effective way to use an objection to make a power play. When used with skill it will close sales for the beginner and the veteran.

You know from experience that an objection is not a turn-down. It is an invitation to use the objection to make a power play that can explode your closing power.

KEY #3: OBTAIN LITTLE CONFIRMATIONS

Obtain little confirmations to explode your closing power. Here's how:

- Select a minor decision which will get a commitment from the customer without his having to say, "I'll buy the whole ball of wax. Go ahead and write the order." You can do this by asking *which,* never *if.* For instance, after you have explained the additional discounts and plus benefits of buying a truck load rather than a number of smaller shipments ask, "Shall we ship this on the first of the month or the fifteenth?" When the customer says "The first," write the order. He has made a painless decision and will be glad to have you consummate the deal so that he (and you) can move on to other things.

There are a great number of little confirmations you can readily use to explode your closing power. Among them:

- **Do you want the net 30 days terms, or do you prefer the 2% ten day terms?**
- **Does the invoice go to your home office or should it be mailed to this address?**
- **Do you want this billed in duplicate?**
- **How should I fill in the shipping address?**
- **Do you prefer the blue color or the cherry red?**
- **Shall I write the order on my book or do you have your own purchase order book?**
- **Are you thinking of our lease plan or do you prefer to own it outright?**
- **Whom shall we name as the beneficiary?**
- **This house meets all your requirements for a home, doesn't it?**
- **Shall we deliver the deluxe model?**
- **Do you like the queen size or the king size?**
- **Do you prefer the chrome wheels and white wall tires?**
- **Will two weeks delivery be soon enough?**

Obtaining little confirmations is a simple way to get the order on the books. It is a simple and proven way to add to the explosive power of your sales closing technique.

KEY #4: HOW TO USE TIE-DOWNS

A tie-down is much like getting a confirmation on a minor point, except that the tie-down is designed more to keep your closed sale intact. There may be a more liberal interpretation of the term in some quarters, but for our purpose we will consider it more as insurance on a hard-earned closed sale. Anything that keeps a closed sale closed has a lot of explosive power.

Here are enough examples to give you the idea.

- Salesman: "Since there are only twelve of this model left, orders are not subject to cancellation. Will you put your name right here please?"
  Customer: "No problem. I don't want to miss out on this deal."

- Salesman: "Our production for the next month must be based on firm orders. Sign by the X please."
  Customer: "O.K."

- Salesman: "A deposit will guarantee delivery. May I have your check for $500 to send in with the order?"
  Customer: "Here it is, but don't wait until Christmas to get it on its way."

Use tie-downs to explode your closing power. Not every customer and not every sale will need to be nailed to the floor, but where the need is apparent, tie your closed sale down. This technique can give a boost to the explosive quality of your closing technique.

KEY #5: ANSWER QUESTIONS WITH QUESTIONS

When you are being pinned to the wall with questions, often you can add to your fire-power by answering with a question. Note these ideas.

- When the prospect or customer asks "How quick can I get delivery?"
  Ask: "How soon do you want delivery?"

- If your customer says, "How much do I have to pay down?"
  Ask: How much can you pay down?"

- When your customer asks, "What kind of quality is this?"
  Ask: "Did you ever see anything better for the money?"

- If your customer asks "How do I know I'll get the goods."
  Ask: "Have you ever heard of my company defaulting?"

Two points worthy of extra attention as you answer a question with a question are these:

- Never answer with a question that will antagonzie your customer or make him look foolish. Keep the tone of your voice friendly and your question designed so that he really answers his own questions when he replies to yours.

- Never ask a question that can be answered negatively. When the customer answers your question negatively he is saying "No." Then you must start your sale all over again.

KEY #6: AVOID CLICHES THAT STEAL FIRE POWER

A cliche is a trite phrase or expression, hackneyed by overuse. It is too weak and feeble to explode your closing power. Cliches are the crutch of lazy salesmen. Leave them for the less ambitious. As a business man intent on using explosive closing power, you will use stronger stuff. By way of illustrating the weakness of selling cliches consider the following:

- "I guarantee that your business will double if you buy my big deal triple-geared automatic widget!"
  Consider: What kind of guarantee is this? Who pays the penalty if the customer's business fails to double? How will this salesman's widget double the man's business? Where is the proof that it will double his business? And how long will it take to double his business?

- "This is the finest quality on the market!"
  Consider: Why is it the finest quality? How is it the finest quality? How will this quality benefit the customer?

- "This is a super product!"
  Consider: Super compared to what? How is it a super product? What will it do for the buyer? What is "super" anyway?

- "Your competition will cry their hearts out when they find out you have my widget!"
  Consider: Why will the competition weep? How will this salesman's widget give his customer such an advantage that the competition will cry? Where are the salesman's facts to support this off-the-cuff claim?

- "This is one more whale of a deal!"
  Consider: "Why is it a whale of a deal? How is it a whale of a deal? What makes it a whale of a deal for the prospect or customer?

Such statements may be well intentioned, but like all cliches, they are more froth than substance. The sophisticated, successful prospect or customer recognizes this.

As an experienced, aggressive salesman or sales executive you will not rely on trite expressions similar to the above. You will use strong, supportive, factual statements that convince your buyers. This will give your closing power explosive force.

KEY #7: HOW TO USE COMMAND POWER TO EXPLODE YOUR CLOSING POWER

Command power is the power to dominate a sales situation. A powerful salesman is always in control though his customer may not so much as be aware of it. He encourages his customer to do a great part of the talking. Still he retains control. He leads the customer or prospect into talking of the business at hand. The interview does not wander astray. The command power of the dominant salesman is aimed at the closed sale.

Command power is not an overbearing, antagonistic selling technique. Command power denotes dominance by clearly and force- fully demonstrating that the salesman is the expert in his field. Command power is the power to exert competence and leadership in such a manner that the customer feels fortunate to have a master salesman who knows what he is talking about and who knows how to get things done. The master salesman is clever enough to lead the customer into agreeing to the closed sale without procrastination. If the customer feels that the whole project was his idea all along, then that is a vibrant sign that the salesman's command power is going full blast.

Check your command power. Listed below are the principal traits of the professional marketing man who uses command power to explode his closing power into a money-making force.

- Self-confidence
- Aggressiveness
- Leadership
- Sincerity
- Knowledge
- Dependability
- Determination
- Success oriented
- Self-reliant
- Firm
- Tactful
- Tough

Sound like a big order to fill? Every one of these traits can be developed, re-inforced, and refined. Men who possess and use these traits are constantly working to improve and strengthen them. There are many examples of such men between the covers of this book and in the field where you work every day. Utilize the techniques and attitudes of such men and watch your command power explode your closing power to exciting heights.

KEY #8: HOW TO <u>INSIST</u> <u>ON</u> <u>AND</u> <u>WIN</u>
THE RIGHT DECISION

If a customer throws you a trial order that is so far from his needs or capacity as to be ridiculous, you do not have a closed sale; you have a sop. A sop is intended to get rid of you before your job is done. Sometimes a trial order produces some beneficial results. Nevertheless, the prudent and logical thing to do is to insist on the right decision. The right decision is the one that delivers to your customer what he wants and needs. Below are time-tested ideas developed and used by today's professional salesmen. These are techniques that insist on and win the right decision day after day.

- Don't accept the first "no" as the end of the sale. Experienced salesmen expect to be turned down five or six times on the average before the customer is lead and pushed into making the right decision. Don't blow it by giving up before your customer or prospect has had a chance to consider all the benefits you can offer.

- Insist on and win the right decision by encouraging your buyer to think positively. Do this with questions designed to produce favorable answers. You can also promote a positive attitude with success stories of other customers in a similar business. Your own enthusiastic attitude also will do much to promote a positive frame of mind.

- Suggest the size of the order yourself. Support your reasoning with customer benefits. When your customer realizes that his interest is at stake, you can insist on the right decision and win it on the spot.

The strong salesman will always insist on the right decision and win it with sound, convincing business tactics. As you pursue this practice your sales closing power will be explosive.

KEY #9: HOW TO MAKE THE CUSTOMER LIKE AGGRESSIVE YOU

Contrary to what the weak-hearted may think, the customer does not cherish the salesman who never asks him to do anything. Why should he? The salesman who never asks his customer to do anything never does anything for his customer.

Thriving business concerns and smart buyers welcome aggressive salesmen. Live wire salesmen are the men who introduce new products, bring new ideas, and spur action. It is no wonder that leading firms often have a rule that every salesman calling on them must be granted an interview within a reasonable time.

Here is a checklist of a portion of the things an aggressive salesman does to explode his closing power. Check your performance against this list and add to it as you develop more and more closing power.

The aggressive salesman:
- Acts as a built-in business consultant to his customers.
- Keeps his buyers updated.
- Introduces new products.
- Shares his merchandising know-how
- Brings his buyers new ideas.
- Emphasizes customer benefits.
- Urges his customers to take action.
- Spreads enthusiasm.
- Does not undersell or oversell.
- Insists on the decision that is right for his customer and for himself.
- Eliminates stagnation in the market place by asking for the order.
- Pushes for the closed sale on every call.

The aggressive salesman builds goodwill by rendering service that reaches beyond the closed sale. He is a businessman who contributes to the success and welfare of his customer. He operates with authority.

When you do the job in an aggressive, helpful manner your customers won't like you — they will love you. And your closing power will explode.

KEY #10: HOW TO MAINTAIN
A STRONG CLOSING POSTURE

The experienced salesman is well aware that he must maintain control of the sales interview from the opening to the closing. Here are some observations gleaned from the experiences and closing methods of professional salesmen and sales executives. These observations are framed to give you a quick reference that will help you maintain a strong closing posture.

- **Don't overdo it.**
  Dominating the sales interview is essential, yes. But it is not the sole consideration. The purpose is to close the sale. Dominance — control — is a part of your closing power. Use it as all smart salesmen do — with polish, courtesy, and business-like firmness. If you overdo it the sales call could become a test of wills with antagonism being the end result.

- **Keep the sales presentation on track.**
  This is where dominance plays its part. You must control the sales presentation. Some buyers purposely break the trend of the interview. Others may be prone to let their mind wander far afield. You can keep the presentation on track and keep your closing posture strong when this happens by:
  - Asking a pointed question that demands a positive statement, simple questions such as: "Isn't this a beautiful texture?" Or, "Did you ever see a grinder that operates on this principle?" can bring your buyer back to the business at hand.
  - Listening attentively until the prospect has talked himself out on the foreign subject. Then you can connect what he has been saying, either directly or indirectly, with the proposition you are selling and regain control. This way you discreetly and effectively maintain dominance.
  - Standing rather than sitting. The salesman who stands up as he works has more room to maneuver, to show samples, to make demonstrations, and to look the customer in the eyes. This is not to say that you should never sit. It is meant to say that standing

often affords the salesman a more commanding position. From this position it is relatively simple to keep your sales presentation on track.

- **Keep the pot boiling.**
The pro never allows his sales presentation to lose momentum. He practices showmanship, plans his presentation, rehearses diligently, and builds a reserve of techniques and methods to keep the pot boiling. When you and your customer are involved in an exciting presentation, your closing posture is always strong.

Finally, the true salesman does not expect every prospect or customer to be sugary sweet. He does not expect to always work in an ideal setting and under painless conditions. Rather, he anticipates and relishes the turmoil, the excitement, and the challenge of the market place. He equips himself to maintain a strong closing posture. He scrupulously uses closing keys that explode his closing power. Then he claims the substantial rewards that are the just due of an enterprising and helpful salesman.

This is your heritage and your responsibility.

Index